React 16 Tooling

Master essential cutting-edge tools, such as
create-react-app, Jest, and Flow

Adam Boduch

BIRMINGHAM - MUMBAI

React 16 Tooling

Acquisition Editors: Ben Renow-Clarke, Suresh M Jain
Project Editor: Suzanne Coutinho
Content Development Editor: Monika Sangwan
Technical Editor: Bhagyashree Rai
Indexer: Mariammal Chettiyar
Proofreader: Tom Jacob
Graphics: Tom Scaria
Production Coordinators: Aparna Bhagat, Sandip Tadge

First published: April 2018

Production reference: 1270418

Published by Packt Publishing Ltd.
Livery Place
35 Livery Street
Birmingham
B3 2PB, UK.

ISBN 978-1-78883-501-5

www.packtpub.com

`mapt.io`

Mapt is an online digital library that gives you full access to over 5,000 books and videos, as well as industry leading tools to help you plan your personal development and advance your career. For more information, please visit our website.

Why subscribe?

- Spend less time learning and more time coding with practical eBooks and Videos from over 4,000 industry professionals

- Improve your learning with Skill Plans built especially for you

- Get a free eBook or video every month

- Mapt is fully searchable

- Copy and paste, print, and bookmark content

PacktPub.com

Did you know that Packt offers eBook versions of every book published, with PDF and ePub files available? You can upgrade to the eBook version at `www.PacktPub.com` and as a print book customer, you are entitled to a discount on the eBook copy. Get in touch with us at `service@packtpub.com` for more details.

At `www.PacktPub.com`, you can also read a collection of free technical articles, sign up for a range of free newsletters, and receive exclusive discounts and offers on Packt books and eBooks.

Contributors

About the author

Adam Boduch has been involved with large-scale JavaScript development for nearly 10 years. Before moving to the frontend, he worked on several large-scale cloud computing products, using Python and Linux. No stranger to complexity, Adam has practical experience with real-world software systems, and the scaling challenges they pose.

He is the author of several JavaScript books, including *React and React Native* published by Packt Publishing, and is passionate about innovative user experiences and high performance.

About the reviewer

Christopher Pitt is an author, speaker, and developer. He spends most of his time learning new technologies and teaching others about them. He has written about topics, including JS game development, PHP framework usage, and how to create simple compilers.

Christopher helped review the chapters on React 16 and Redux in *React 16 Essentials - Second Edition* published by Packt Publishing.

Packt is searching for authors like you

If you're interested in becoming an author for Packt, please visit `authors.packtpub.com` and apply today. We have worked with thousands of developers and tech professionals, just like you, to help them share their insight with the global tech community. You can make a general application, apply for a specific hot topic that we are recruiting an author for, or submit your own idea.

Table of Contents

Preface

Any given technology is only as good as the tooling that supports it. React is no exception. Although React is just a library from creating user interfaces, the ecosystem that has sprung up around it means that a typical React project has many moving parts. Without the appropriate tooling, you end up spending a lot of time manually performing tasks that would be better off automated by a tool.

React tools come in many forms. Some have been around for a while, others are brand new. Some are found in the browser, others are strictly command line. There are a lot of tools that React developers can use—I've tried to focus on the most powerful tools that have had a direct impact on projects that I've worked on.

Each chapter of this book focuses one React tool. It starts with basic development tools, moves into tools that aid with perfecting your React component design, and finishes with tools for deploying React applications in production.

Who this book is for

This book is intended for React developers who are constantly on the lookout for better tools and techniques to up their game. While React experience isn't a strict requirement for reading this book, you'll get the most value if you understand some of the basics of React beforehand.

What this book covers

Chapter 1, *Creating a Personalized React Development Ecosystem*, introduces the motivations for tooling in React projects.

Chapter 2, *Efficiently Bootstrapping React Applications with Create React App*, gets you up and running with `create-react-app`.

Chapter 3, *Development Mode and Mastering Hot Reloading*, shows you how to develop your React application using a development server and hot module reloading.

Chapter 4, *Optimizing Test-Driven React Development*, teaches you how to incorporate Jest unit testing into your project.

Chapter 5, *Streamlining Development and Refactoring with Type-Safe React Components*, introduces type-safety with React components using Flow.

Chapter 6, *Enforcing Code Quality to Improve Maintainability*, gets you started with ESLint and Prettier—tools for enhancing the quality of your code.

Chapter 7, *Isolating Components with Storybook*, shows you have to isolate component development from the rest of your application using Storybook.

Chapter 8, *Debugging Components in the Browser*, goes into depth on the React Development Tools browser plugin to assist with React component debugging.

Chapter 9, *Instrumenting Application State with Redux*, introduces the Redux DevTools browser plugin, providing you with a clear picture of your application state.

Chapter 10, *Building and Deploying Static React Sites with Gatsby*, teaches you how to create static websites using Gatsby and React components.

Chapter 11, *Building and Deploying React Applications with Docker Containers*, shows you how to deploy production-ready React applications to containers.

To get the most out of this book

- Learn the basics of React.
- If you're already using React in your project, identify missing tools.

Download the example code files

You can download the example code files for this book from your account at www.packtpub.com. If you purchased this book elsewhere, you can visit www.packtpub.com/support and register to have the files emailed directly to you.

You can download the code files by following these steps:

1. Log in or register at www.packtpub.com.
2. Select the **SUPPORT** tab.
3. Click on **Code Downloads & Errata**.
4. Enter the name of the book in the **Search** box and follow the onscreen instructions.

Once the file is downloaded, please make sure that you unzip or extract the folder using the latest version of:

- WinRAR/7-Zip for Windows
- Zipeg/iZip/UnRarX for Mac
- 7-Zip/PeaZip for Linux

The code bundle for the book is also hosted on GitHub at `https://github.com/PacktPublishing/React-16-Tooling`. In case there's an update to the code, it will be updated on the existing GitHub repository.

We also have other code bundles from our rich catalog of books and videos available at `https://github.com/PacktPublishing/`. Check them out!

Download the color images

We also provide a PDF file that has color images of the screenshots/diagrams used in this book. You can download it here: `http://www.packtpub.com/sites/default/files/downloads/React16Tooling_ColorImages.pdf`.

Conventions used

There are a number of text conventions used throughout this book.

`CodeInText`: Indicates code words in text, database table names, folder names, filenames, file extensions, pathnames, dummy URLs, user input, and Twitter handles. Here is an example: "Next, let's look at the `package.json` file that was created by *Create React App*."

A block of code is set as follows:

```
import React from 'react';

const Heading = ({ children }) => (
  <h1>{children}</h1>
);

export default Heading;
```

When we wish to draw your attention to a particular part of a code block, the relevant lines or items are set in bold:

```
import React from 'react';

const Heading = ({ children }) => (
  <h1>{children}</h1>
);

export default Heading;
```

Any command-line input or output is written as follows:

```
$ npm install -g create-react-app
```

Bold: Indicates a new term, an important word, or words that you see onscreen. For example, words in menus or dialog boxes appear in the text like this. Here is an example: "Once you click on the **Add extension** button, the extension is marked as installed."

 Warnings or important notes appear like this.

 Tips and tricks appear like this.

Get in touch

Feedback from our readers is always welcome.

General feedback: Email `feedback@packtpub.com` and mention the book title in the subject of your message. If you have questions about any aspect of this book, please email us at `questions@packtpub.com`.

Errata: Although we have taken every care to ensure the accuracy of our content, mistakes do happen. If you have found a mistake in this book, we would be grateful if you would report this to us. Please visit `www.packtpub.com/submit-errata`, selecting your book, clicking on the Errata Submission Form link, and entering the details.

Piracy: If you come across any illegal copies of our works in any form on the Internet, we would be grateful if you would provide us with the location address or website name. Please contact us at copyright@packtpub.com with a link to the material.

If you are interested in becoming an author: If there is a topic that you have expertise in and you are interested in either writing or contributing to a book, please visit authors.packtpub.com.

Reviews

Please leave a review. Once you have read and used this book, why not leave a review on the site that you purchased it from? Potential readers can then see and use your unbiased opinion to make purchase decisions, we at Packt can understand what you think about our products, and our authors can see your feedback on their book. Thank you!

For more information about Packt, please visit packtpub.com.

1
Creating a Personalized React Development Ecosystem

When people hear React, they think of a focused library used for efficiently rendering user interfaces. When people hear framework, they think of a large system that might have a few useful tools within it but is otherwise a bloated mess. They're correct about frameworks for the most part, but saying that React isn't a framework is a little misleading.

If you take React out of the box and try to do any meaningful development with it, you'll promptly hit a wall. This is because instead of being distributed as a monolithic framework, React is better described as a core library surrounded by an ecosystem of tools.

The advantage of a framework is that you can install the core library along with the supported tooling in one shot. The downside is that every project is different and you can't be sure what tools you need versus those that you won't. Another advantage to having an ecosystem of tools is that they can evolve independently from one another; you don't have to wait for a new release of the entire framework to get an enhancement for one of the tools that your project uses.

The aim of this book is to show you how to best utilize the tooling ecosystem surrounding React. In this chapter, you'll be introduced to the concept of React tooling by learning the following:

- React without tooling
- Introduction to tooling
- The tools covered in this book
- Deciding which tools are needed for your project

What's included with React

Before we dive into tooling discussions, let's make sure that we're on the same page about what React is, and what actually comes with the package when you install it. There are two core React packages required for running React web applications. We'll take a look at these now to provide you with some context for thinking about React tooling.

Components that compare render trees

The first part of the React core is the package called `react`. This package is what we interface with directly when writing React components. It's a small API—the only time we really use it is when we're creating components with state and we need to extend the `Component` class.

There's a lot going on under the hood with the `react` package. This is where the render tree resides and is responsible for efficiently rendering UI elements. Another name for the render tree is the virtual DOM. The idea is that you only have to write JSX markup that describe the UI elements that you want to render while the render tree takes care of everything else:

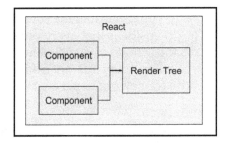

What you see in this diagram are the components that your code directly interfaces with, and the render tree that takes care of handling presentational changes that result from components that change state. The render tree and everything that it does for you is the key value proposition of React.

The DOM render target

The second part of the React core is the **Document Object Model** (**DOM**) itself. In fact, the name virtual DOM is rooted in the idea that React is creating DOM representations in JavaScript before it actually talks to the DOM APIs. However, the render tree is a better name because React is creating an **AST** (short for **Abstract Syntax Tree**) based on the React components and their states. This is why the same React library is able to work with projects like React Native.

The `react-dom` package is used to actually translate the render tree into DOM elements in the browser by directly communicating with the browser DOM APIs. Here's what the previous diagram looks like with `react-dom` included:

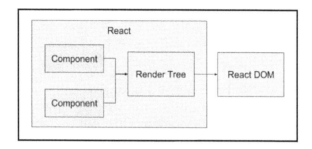

This is a nice architecture—it means that you can substitute `react-dom` for another render target with little effort. As you can see, the core layer of React is minimal. No wonder it's so popular—we can create user interfaces with declarative code that are easy to maintain and are efficient with little effort on our part. With this in mind, let's shift our focus over to the tooling that makes all of this possible.

Introducing tooling?

Tooling isn't unique to React. Every project has its own set of tools that handle tasks related to the core technology so that you don't have to. With frameworks, tooling is baked into the project for the most part. With libraries like React, you get to choose the tools you need versus those that don't play a role in your project.

Now that you know what the React core is, what makes up the rest of the React ecosystem?

Ancillary tasks outside of React

Framework bloat is a major turn-off for a lot of people. The reason it feels like bloat is because they have a lot of features that you'll likely never use. React handles this well because it has a clear distinction between the core library and anything else, including things that are essential for React development.

There are two observations I've made about React and the way it's positioned within its surrounding ecosystem:

- It's easier to deploy apps that depend on a simple library instead of a framework where all batteries are included
- It's easier to think about application development when you have tools that stay out of the way for the most part

In other words, you don't have to use the majority of React tools, but some of them are incredibly helpful.

Any given tool is external to the library you're working with; it's essential to remember this. Tools exist to automate something that would otherwise suck more development time out of our lives. Life is too short to manually do things that can be done for us. I repeat, life is too short for tasks that software can perform better than us. If you're a React developer, take comfort in the fact that there are tools out there for all of the important things that you need to do but don't have time to do.

A construction site analogy

Perhaps, the ultimate motivator for taking tooling seriously is thinking about what life would be like without the tools that we depend on as professionals. The construction industry is more mature than software and serves as a great example.

Imagine that you are part of a team that's responsible for building a house—an immensely complex undertaking with many moving parts. Now, think about everything that you have to work with. Let's start with the materials themselves. Anything that doesn't have to be assembled on site, isn't. When you're building a house, many components show up partially assembled. For example, sections of roof framing or mixed cement shows up when it's needed.

Then there are actual tools that builders use when putting the house together—simple screwdrivers, hammers, and measuring tapes are taken for granted. What would construction life be like without the ability to create components offsite or the availability of tools to work with everyday construction materials? Would it make the construction of a house impossible? No. Would the process of building it become some unbearably expensive and slow that it'd likely be cancelled before completed? Yes.

Unfortunately, in the software world, we're only beginning to understand how important tooling is. It doesn't matter that we have all the materials and knowledge to build the house of the future. If we don't have the right tooling, it might never be built.

React tooling covered in this book

There are literally hundreds of React tools in existence today. The aim of this book, however, is to cover the essential tools for React development. Even with the curated list of tools that you'll learn about in this book, you probably won't use every single one in any given project. Let's take a brief look at the tooling that we'll be looking at throughout the remainder of this book.

JSX needs to be compiled to JavaScript

React uses a special syntax that resembles HTML to declare components. This markup, called JSX, is embedded in the component JavaScript and needs to be compiled to JavaScript before it's usable by the browser.

The most common approach is to use Babel—a JavaScript compiler—along with a JSX plugin:

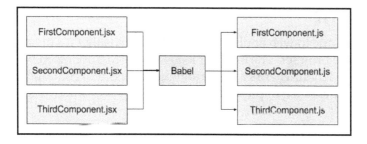

The trick is finding a way to make this compilation step as seamless as possible. As a developer, you shouldn't need to concern yourself with the JavaScript output produced by Babel.

Newer JavaScript language features need to be transpiled

Similar to compiling JSX to JavaScript, newer JavaScript language features need to be compiled into versions that are widely supported by browsers everywhere. In fact, once you figure out how to compile JSX to JavaScript, the same process is used to transpile between different versions of JavaScript:

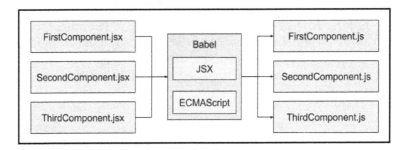

You shouldn't have to worry about the transformed output of your JSX or JavaScript compilation. These are activities better suited for tools to handle, so that you can focus on application development.

Hot module loading to enable application development

Something that's unique to web application development is that it's mostly static content that's loaded into the browser. The browser loads the HTML, followed by any scripts which are then run to completion. There's a long-running process that continuously refreshes the page based on the state of the application—everything is over a network.

As you can imagine, this is especially annoying during development when you want the see the results of your code changes as they're introduced. You don't want to have to manually refresh the page every time you do something. This is where hot module replacement comes into play. Essentially, HMR is a tool that listens for code changes, and when it detects one, it sends a new version of the module to the browser:

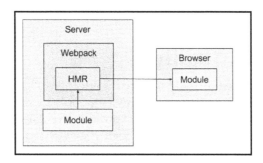

Even with a tool like Webpack and its HMR component, it's time-consuming and error-prone to get this setup working correctly, even for simple React projects. Thankfully, there's tooling that hides these setup details from developers today.

Running unit tests automatically

You know that you need to write tests for your components. It's not that you don't want to write the actual tests; it's that setting them up so that they're able to run can be a pain. The Jest unit test tool simplifies this because it knows where tests can be found and can run them:

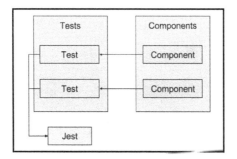

With Jest, we have a place where all of our unit tests go, and each depend on the component that they're testing. This tool knows where to find these tests and how to run them. The result is that we get nice unit test and code coverage output when we need it. There is no overhead beyond actually writing the tests.

Thinking about type safety

JavaScript isn't a type-safe language. Type safety can vastly improve the quality of applications by eliminating the possibility of runtime errors. Once again, we can use tooling to make type-safe React applications. The Flow tool can examine your code, look for type annotations, and notify you when errors are found.

Linting for code quality

It's one thing to have an application that works; it's another to have an application that works and has maintainable code that doesn't make people's eyes bleed. The best way to achieve measurable code quality is to adopt a standard, like Airbnb's (`https://github.com/airbnb/javascript`). The best way to enforce coding standards is to use a linter. With React applications, the preferred linting tool is ESLint (`https://eslint.org/`).

Isolating component development environments

Perhaps the most overlooked tool of React developers is Storybook, which is used for isolated component development. You don't realize it until you're developing your component, but the application can get in the way. Sometimes, you just want to see how the component looks and behaves all on its own:

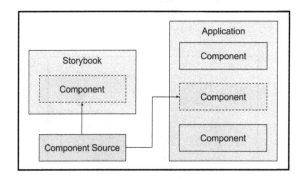

With a tool like Storybook, it's trivial to provide an isolated context for your component, free of distractions from other components.

Providing a browser-based debugging environment

Sometimes, looking at unit test output and source code isn't enough to figure out a problem that you're experiencing. Instead, you need to see what's going on as you interact with the application itself. In the browser, you install React tooling that makes it easy to inspect React components as they are related to rendered HTML content.

React also has some built-in performance monitoring capabilities that extend the abilities of the browser developer tools. You can use them to examine and profile your components at a low level.

Deploying React applications

When you're ready to deploy your React application, it isn't as simple as producing a build and distributing it. In fact, you might not even distribute it at all if you're building a hosted service. Regardless of what the end use case of your application is, there are likely going to be several moving parts in addition to the React frontend. Increasingly, containerizing the main processes that make up your application stack is the preferred approach:

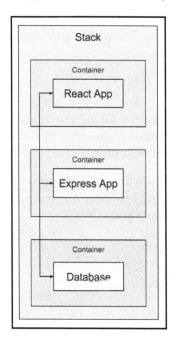

In order to create and deploy React application stacks like this, you'll rely on tools like Docker, especially when it comes time to automate the various deployment scenarios of your project.

Choosing the right tools

If the tooling in the preceding section seemed like a bit much for a single project, don't sweat it. Trying to leverage every possible React tool at the same time is always a mistake. Address one problem at a time, starting with the essentials. As your project moves forward, add in the optional tools to expand your toolset.

Essential tools

There are some React tools that you simply can't live without. For example, browsers don't understand JSX syntax, so this needs to be compiled to JavaScript. As you write code, you'll want to lint it to make sure that basic mistakes aren't missed, and you'll want to run your unit tests. If you try hard enough, you might be able to get by without these tools. But that's the thing—you would spend more effort not using a given tool than to simply embrace it.

As a starting point, find the minimal set of React tools that allow you to make progress. Once your progress noticeably slows, it's time to consider introducing additional tools.

Optional tools

Optional tools are things that you might not get any real value from. For example, you probably won't reap enormous benefits from using Flow to check for type safety or Storybook to isolate component development at the very beginning of a project.

The key thing to remember is that any React tool is optional, and no decisions are permanent. You can always bring in Flow later on, and you can always ditch Storybook if isolated component development isn't your thing.

Summary

This chapter introduced you to the concept of tooling in the React ecosystem. You learned that React, at its core, is a simple library and that it depends on the use of several tools to be of any value in the real world. Frameworks try to provide all of the tooling that you'll ever need for your project. While convenient, the needs of the framework users are difficult to predict and can be a distraction from core functionality.

Next, you learned that tooling in React can be a challenge because as a React developer, you're responsible for choosing the right tools and managing their configuration. You then got an overview of the tooling that you'll learn about in more detail throughout the remainder of this book. Lastly, you learned that some tools are critical for React development and you'll need to get them set up right away. Others are optional, and you might not start using them till there's an actual need later on in the life of the project.

In the next chapter, you'll use the *Create React App* tool to bootstrap a React project.

2
Efficiently Bootstrapping React Applications with Create React App

The first React tool you'll learn about in this book is *Create React App*. It is a command-line utility that helps you, surprisingly, create a React application. This might sound like something that you shouldn't need much help doing, but when you use this tool, there's a lot of configuration that you no longer have to think about. In this chapter, you'll learn:

- Installing the *Create React App* tool on your system
- Bootstraping the creation of your React app
- What packages are installed when you create a new application
- The directory organization and files created with your application

Installing Create React App

The first step is installing *Create React App*, which is an npm package: `create-react-app`. This package should be installed globally because it installs a command on your system that's used to create your React projects. In other words, `create-react-app` isn't actually part of your React project—it's used to initialize your React project.

Here's how you can install *Create React App* globally:

```
$ npm install -g create-react-app
```

Notice the `-g` flag in the command—this makes sure that the `create-react-app` command is installed globally. Once the installation is complete, you can make sure that the command is good to go by running the following:

```
$ create-react-app -V
```

```
> 1.4.1
```

Now you're ready to use this tool to create your first React app!

Creating your first app

We'll spend the remainder of the chapter creating your first React application with *Create React App*. Don't worry, this is super easy to do, so it'll be a short chapter. The goal of *Create React App* is to start building features for your application as soon as possible. You cannot do this if you're sinking time into configuring your system.

Create React App provides what's called a **zero configuration app**. This means that we supply the name of the app, then it'll go install the dependencies that we need, and create the boilerplate directory structure and files for us. Let's get started.

Specifying a project name

The only configuration value that you need to supply to *Create React App* so that it can bootstrap your project is the name. This is specified as an argument to the `create-react-app` command:

```
$ create-react-app my-react-app
```

This will create a `my-react-app` directory in your current directory, if it doesn't already exist. If it already exists, the directory will be used. This is where you'll find everything to do with your application. Once the directory is created, it installs package dependencies and creates project directories and files. Here's a shortened version of what the `create-react-app` command output might look like:

```
Creating a new React app in 02/my-react-app.
Installing packages. This might take a couple of minutes.
Installing react, react-dom, and react-scripts...
+ react-dom@16.0.0
+ react@16.0.0
+ react-scripts@1.0.14
added 1272 packages in 57.831s
Success! Created my-react-app at 02/my-react-app
Inside that directory, you can run several commands:
  npm start
    Starts the development server.
  npm run build
    Bundles the app into static files for production.
  npm test
    Starts the test runner.
  npm run eject
    Removes this tool and copies build dependencies,
    configuration files and scripts into the app directory.
    If you do this, you can't go back!
We suggest that you begin by typing:
  cd my-react-app
  npm start
Happy hacking!
```

This output shows you a number of interesting things. First, it shows which things were installed. Second, it shows you the commands available for you to run in your project. You'll learn how to use each of these commands throughout this book, starting with the next chapter. For now, let's take a look at the project that you just created and see what it contains.

Automatic dependency handling

Let's take a look at the dependencies that were installed as part of the bootstrapping process. You can list your projects packages by running npm ls --depth=0. The --depth=0 option means that you only want to see the top-level dependencies:

```
├────── react@16.0.0
├────── react-dom@16.0.0
└────── react-scripts@1.0.14
```

There isn't much here, just the two core React libraries that you need, and something called react-scripts. This latter package contains the scripts that you'll want to run with this project such as starting the development server and making a production build.

Next, let's look at the package.json file that was created by *Create React App*:

```json
{
  "name": "my-react-app",
  "version": "0.1.0",
  "private": true,
  "dependencies": {
    "react": "^16.0.0",
    "react-dom": "^16.0.0",
    "react-scripts": "1.0.14"
  },
  "scripts": {
    "start": "react-scripts start",
    "build": "react-scripts build",
    "test": "react-scripts test --env=jsdom",
    "eject": "react-scripts eject"
  }
}
```

Here is where dependencies are tracked, so that you can install your app on different machines that don't have *Create React App* on them. You can see that the dependencies section matches the output of the npm ls --depth=0 command. The scripts section specifies the commands available to run with this project. These are all react-scripts commands—react-scripts is installed as a dependency.

One of the more powerful aspects of *Create React App* is that it simplifies this package.json configuration for you. Instead of having dozens of dependencies that you have to maintain yourself, you have less than a handful of dependencies. The react-scripts package handles the dynamic configuration aspect for you.

For example, when you run a React development server, you typically have to spend a lot of time messing around with Webpack configuration and making sure that the appropriate Babel plugins are installed. Since `react-scripts` creates a standard configuration for these things on the fly, you don't have to worry about it. Instead, you can start writing application code write away.

The `react-scripts` package also handles much of the dependencies that you would normally have to handle yourself. You can use `npm ls --depth=1` to get an idea of what dependencies this package takes care of for you:

```
└──┬ react-scripts@1.0.14
   ├── autoprefixer@7.1.2
   ├── babel-core@6.25.0
   ├── babel-eslint@7.2.3
   ├── babel-jest@20.0.3
   ├── babel-loader@7.1.1
   ├── babel-preset-react-app@3.0.3
   ├── babel-runtime@6.26.0
   ├── case-sensitive-paths-webpack-plugin@2.1.1
   ├── chalk@1.1.3
   ├── css-loader@0.28.4
   ├── dotenv@4.0.0
   ├── eslint@4.4.1
   ├── eslint-config-react-app@2.0.1
   ├── eslint-loader@1.9.0
   ├── eslint-plugin-flowtype@2.35.0
   ├── eslint-plugin-import@2.7.0
   ├── eslint-plugin-jsx-a11y@5.1.1
   ├── eslint-plugin-react@7.1.0
   ├── extract-text-webpack-plugin@3.0.0
   ├── file-loader@0.11.2
   ├── fs-extra@3.0.1
   ├── fsevents@1.1.2
   ├── html-webpack-plugin@2.29.0
   ├── jest@20.0.4
   ├── object-assign@4.1.1 deduped
   ├── postcss-flexbugs-fixes@3.2.0
   ├── postcss-loader@2.0.6
   ├── promise@8.0.1
   ├── react-dev-utils@4.1.0
   ├── style-loader@0.18.2
```

```
├──── sw-precache-webpack-plugin@0.11.4
├──── url-loader@0.5.9
├──── webpack@3.5.1
├──── webpack-dev-server@2.8.2
├──── webpack-manifest-plugin@1.2.1
└──── whatwg-fetch@2.0.3
```

Typically, you wouldn't interact with most of these packages in your application code. When you have to actively manage dependencies that you don't directly use, it can feel like a huge time sink. *Create React App* helps squash this feeling.

Directory structure

At this point, you have an understanding of the dependencies that are installed as part of your project when you create it using *Create React App*. In addition to the dependencies, *Create React App* sets up some other boilerplate files and directories. Let's go over these quickly so that you can start coding in the following chapter.

Top-level files

There are only two files created in the top level of your application that you need to worry about:

- README.md: This Markdown file is used to describe the project. It's a great place to explain why your project exists and how people can get started with it, especially if you plan on making your app a GitHub project.
- package.json: This file is used to configure all aspects of distributing your application as an npm package. For example, this is where you can add new dependencies or remove obsolete dependencies. This file is key if you plan on publishing your app to the main npm registry.

Static assets

Create React App creates a public directory for you with a few files in it. This is where static application assets go. It contains the following by default:

- `favion.ico`: This is the React logo that gets displayed in browser tabs. You'll want to replace this with something representative of your application before you ship.
- `index.html`: This is the HTML file that's served to browsers and the entry point of your React application.
- `manifest.json`: This is used by some mobile operating systems when the application is added to the home screen.

Source code

The `src` directory created by `create-react-app` is the most important part of your application. This is where any React components you create will live. Out of the box, this directory has some source files in it to get you on your way, though you'll obviously replace the majority of them as you move forward. Here's what you'll find by default:

- `App.css`: This defines some simple CSS to style the `App` component
- `App.js`: This is the default component that renders the application HTML
- `App.test.js`: This is a basic test for the `App` component
- `index.css`: This defines application-wide styles
- `index.js`: This is the entry point into your application—renders the `App` component
- `logo.svg`: An animated React logo that's rendered by the `App` component
- `registerServiceWorker.js`: In production builds, this enables loading components from an offline cache

There are two benefits to having these default source files created for you. First, you can quickly start the application to make sure everything is working and that you didn't make any basic mistakes. Second, it sets a basic pattern for you to follow with your components. Throughout this book, you'll see how applying patterns to components actually aids with tooling.

Summary

In this chapter, you learned how to install the *Create React App* tool on your system. *Create React App* is the tool of choice for bootstrapping modern React applications. The goal of *Create React App* is to have developers go from nothing to creating React components in minimal time.

Once this tool was installed, you created your first React app using it. The only piece of configuration you had to provide was the application name. Once the tool finished installing dependencies and creating boilerplate files and directories, you were ready to start writing code.

Then, we looked at `react-scripts` and the dependencies that this package takes care of for you. You were then taken on a whirlwind tour of the overall structure of the application that was created for you.

In the following chapter, we'll start developing some React components. To do this, we'll fire up the development server. You'll also learn how to get up and running with a `create-react-app` development environment.

3
Development Mode and Mastering Hot Reloading

In the previous chapter, you learned how to use `create-react-app`. This is just the beginning of our *React tooling* journey. By using `create-react-app` to bootstrap your application, you're installing many other tools used for development. These tools are part of the `react-scripts` package. The focus of this chapter will be the development server that comes with `react-scripts` where we'll cover:

- Starting the development server
- Automatic Webpack configuration
- Putting hot component reloading to use

Starting the development server

If you created a React application using the `create-react-app` tool in the previous chapter, then you have everything you need to launch a development server. No configuration is necessary! Let's start it up right now. First, make sure that you're in the project directory:

```
cd my-react-app/
```

Now you can start the development server:

```
npm start
```

This will start the development server using the `start` script from the `react-scripts` package. You should see the console output that looks like this:

```
Compiled successfully!
You can now view my-react-app in the browser.
  Local:            http://localhost:3000/
  On Your Network:  http://192.168.86.101:3000/
Note that the development build is not optimized.
To create a production build, use npm run build.
```

You'll notice that in addition to printing this output in the console, this script will launch a new browser tab with `http://localhost:3000/` as the address. The page that's displayed looks like this:

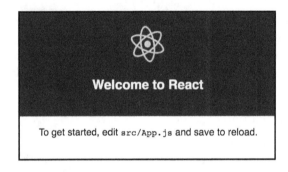

We've accomplished a lot in just a couple of chapters so far. Let's pause and recap what we've done:

1. You created a new React application using the `create-react-app` package.
2. You have the basic project structure in place and a placeholder `App` component to render.
3. You launched the development server, and now you're ready building React components.

To get to this point without `create-react-app` and `react-scripts` would typically take hours. You probably don't have hours to spend messing with meta development work. A lot of it has just been automated for you!

Webpack configuration

Webpack is the tool of choice for building modern web applications. It's powerful enough to compile everything from JSX syntax to static images into bundles that are ready to deploy. It also comes with a development server. Its main drawback is its complexity. There are a lot of moving parts that need to be configured just to get Webpack off the ground, but you didn't have to touch any of it. This is because most of the Webpack configuration values that you would set for a React app are the same for most React apps.

There are two separate pieces of the development server to configure. First, there's the Webpack development server itself. Then, there's the main Webpack configuration, which you'll need even if you weren't using the Webpack development server. So where are these configuration files? They're part of the `react-scripts` package, meaning, you don't have to mess around with them!

Let's walk through some of these configuration values now to give you a better sense of the unnecessary headache you're able to avoid.

Entry points

Entry points are used to tell Webpack where to start looking for modules used to build your application. With a simple application, you don't need anything more than a single file as your entry point. For example, this could be your `index.js` file that's used to render your root React component. Another way to think of this entry point, borrowing terminology from other programming languages, is the main program.

The `react-scripts` package looks for an `index.js` file in your source folder when you run the `start` script. It adds a couple of other entry points as well:

- Polyfills for `Promise`, `fetch()`, and `Object.assign()`. These are only used if they don't already exist in the target browser.
- A client for hot module reloading.

These last two entry points are valuable for React development, but they're not something you want to have to think about when you're trying to get a project off the ground.

Build output

The job of Webpack is to bundle your application resources so that they can be easily served from the web. This means that you have to configure various things related to bundle output, starting with the output path and file. The Webpack development server doesn't actually write a bundle file to disk because it is assumed that builds will happen frequently. The resulting bundle is kept in memory. Even with this in mind, you still have to configure the main output path because the Webpack development server still needs to serve it to the browser as though it were a real file.

In addition to the main output location, you can also configure chunk filenames and the public path used to serve files from. Chunks are bundles that are split into smaller pieces to avoid creating a single bundle file that's too big and might cause performance problems. Wait, what? Thinking about performance and the path used to serve resources before you've even implemented a single component for your application? This is completely unnecessary at this point in the project. Don't worry, `react-scripts` has you covered and provides configuration for output that you probably won't ever need to change.

Resolving input files

One of the key strengths of Webpack is that you don't need to supply it with a list of modules that need to be bundled. Once you supply an entry point in the Webpack configuration, it can figure out which modules your application needs, and will bundle them accordingly. Needless to say, this is a complex task that Webpack is performing for you and needs all the help it can get.

For example, part of the `resolve` configuration is telling Webpack which file extensions to consider, for example, `.js` or `.jsx`. You also want to tell Webpack where to look for package modules. These are modules that you didn't write and aren't part of your application. These are npm packages that are typically found in the `node_modules` directory of your project.

There are more advanced options as well, such as creating aliases for modules and using resolver plugins. Once again, none of these things are relevant to you before you write any React code, yet, you need them configured so that you can develop your components, unless of course, you're using `react-scripts` to take care of this configuration for you.

Loading and compiling files

Loading and compiling files for your bundle are probably the most important capabilities of Webpack. Interestingly, Webpack doesn't directly process your files once they're loaded. Instead, it coordinates I/O as it passes through Webpack loader plugins. For example, the Webpack configuration used by `react-scripts` uses the following loader plugins:

- **Babel**: The Babel loader transpiles the JavaScript in your application's source files into JavaScript that all browsers will understand. Babel will also take care of compiling your JSX syntax into regular JavaScript.
- **CSS**: There are a couple loaders used by `react-scripts` that result in CSS output:
    - `style-loader`: Import CSS modules like JavaScript modules using the `import` syntax.
    - `postcss-loader`: Enhanced CSS features like modules, functions, and custom properties.
- **Images**: Images that are imported by JavaScript or CSS are bundled using `url-loader`.

As your application matures, you might find yourself needing to load and bundle different types of assets that fall outside of the default `react-scripts` configuration. Since you don't need to worry about this at the beginning of your project, there's no point in wasting time configuring Webpack loaders.

Configuring plugins

There's a seemingly infinite list of plugins that you can add to your Webpack configuration. Some of them are really useful for development, so you want these plugins configured up front. Others might not prove useful until down the road as your project matures. The plugins that `react-scripts` uses out of the box contribute to a seamless React development experience.

Hot reloading

The hot module reloading mechanism requires configuration in both the main Webpack bundle configuration file, as well as the development server configuration. This is another example of something that you want as soon as you start developing your components, but don't want to spend time on. The `start` command of `react-scripts` starts a Webpack development server with hot reloading configured and ready to go.

Hot component reloading in action

Earlier in this chapter, you learned how to start the `react-scripts` development server. This development server has hot module reloading configured and ready to use. All you have to do is start writing component code.

Let's start by implementing the following heading component:

```
import React from 'react';

const Heading = ({ children }) => (
  <h1>{children}</h1>
);

export default Heading;
```

This component will render any child text as an `<h1>` tag. Easy enough? Now, let's change the `App` component to use `Heading`:

```
import React, { Component } from 'react';
import './App.css';
import Heading from './Heading';

class App extends Component {
  render() {
    return (
      <div className="App">
        <Heading>
          My App
        </Heading>
      </div>
    );
  }
}

export default App;
```

Then, you can see what this looks like:

The `Heading` component is rendered as expected. Now that you've initially loaded your application in the browser, it's time to put the hot reloading mechanism to work. Let's say that you've decided to change the title of this heading:

```
<Heading>
  My App Heading
</Heading>
```

As soon as you hit save in your code editor, the Webpack development server detects that a change has taken place and that new code should be compiled, bundled, and sent to the browser. Since `react-scripts` has taken care of configuring Webpack, you can just head right into the browser and watch the changes as they take place:

This should help speed up development! In fact, it already has and you've just witnessed it. You altered the text of a React element and saw the result immediately. You could have spent hours setting up this infrastructure with Webpack configuration at the center of it, but you didn't have to because you just reused the configuration provided by `react-scripts` because nearly all React development configurations should look about the same. Over time they diverge, but projects without any components look awfully similar. The name of the game is to hit the ground running.

Now let's try something different. Let's add a component with `state` and see what happens when we change it. Here's a simple button component that keeps track of its clicks:

```
import React, { Component } from 'react';

class Button extends Component {
  style = {}

  state = {
    count: 0
  }

  onClick = () => this.setState(state => ({
    count: state.count + 1
  }));

  render() {
    const { count } = this.state;
    const {
      onClick,
      style
    } = this;

    return (
      <button {...{ onClick, style }}>
        Clicks: {count}
      </button>
    );
  }
}

export default Button;
```

Let's break down what's happening with this component:

1. It has a `style` object, but without any properties, so this has no effect.
2. It has a `count` state that is incremented each time the button is clicked.
3. The `onClick()` handler sets the new `count` state, incrementing the old `count` state by 1.
4. The `render()` method renders a `<button>` element with an `onClick` handler and a `style` property.

Once you click on this button, it will have a new state. How will this work with hot module loading? Let's try it out. We'll render this `Button` component in our `App` component as follows:

```
import React, { Component } from 'react';
import './App.css';
import Heading from './Heading';
import Button from './Button';

class App extends Component {
  render() {
    return (
      <div className="App">
        <Heading>
          My App Heading
        </Heading>
        <Button/>
      </div>
    );
  }
}

export default App;
```

When you load the UI, you should see something like this:

My App Heading

Clicks: 0

Clicking on the button should increment the `count` state by 1. Sure enough, clicking it a few times causes the rendered button label to change, reflecting the new state:

My App Heading

Clicks: 3

Now, let's say that you wanted to change the style of the button. We'll make the text bold:

```
class Button extends Component {
  style = { fontWeight: 'bold' }

  . . .

  render() {
    const { count } = this.state;
    const {
      onClick,
      style
    } = this;

    return (
      <button {...{ onClick, style }}>
        Clicks: {count}
      </button>
    );
  }
}

export default Button;
```

The hot module mechanism works as expected, but with one important difference: the state of the `Button` component has reverted to its initial state:

This happens because when the `Button.js` module is replaced, the existing component instance is unmounted before being replaced with the new instance. The state of the component is blown away along with the component itself.

The solution to this is to use the *React Hot Loader* tool. This tool will keep your components mounted as their implementation is updated. This means that the state persists. In some cases, this can be incredibly helpful. Is this needed when you're just getting started? Probably not—hot module reloading that doesn't persist state is good enough to get rolling.

Ejecting from Create React App

The goal of `create-react-app` and `react-scripts` is zero-configuration React development. The less time you spend configuring development boilerplate, the more time you spend developing components. You should continue to avoid worrying about configuring your app for as long as you can. But at some point, you'll have to bail on `create-react-app` and maintain your own configuration.

Providing a zero-configuration environment is only possible because many defaults and many limitations are assumed by `create-react-app`. This is the trade-off. By providing sane defaults for most of the things that React developers have to do but don't want to, you're making a choice for the developer. This is a good thing—being able to punt on decisions early in the development of your application makes you more productive.

React component hot loading is a good example of a limitation of `create-react-app`. It isn't part of the configuration offered by `create-react-app` because you probably don't need it early on in your project. But as things become more complex, being able to troubleshoot your components without disrupting their current state is critical. At this point in the project, `create-react-app` has served its purpose and it's time to eject.

To eject from `create-react-app`, run the `eject` script:

```
npm run eject
```

You'll be asked to confirm this action, because there's no going back. At this point, it's worth reinforcing the point that you should not eject from `create-react-app` until it gets in the way. Remember, once you eject from `create-react-app`, you now assume the responsibilities of maintaining all of the scripts and all of the configuration that was once hidden from view.

The good news is that part of the ejection process involves setting up scripts and configuration values for your project. Essentially, it's the same thing that `react-scripts` uses internally, except now these scripts and config files are copied into your project directory for you to maintain. For example, after ejecting, you'll see a `scripts` directory with the following files:

- `build.js`
- `start.js`
- `test.js`

Now if you take a look at `package.json`, you'll see that the scripts that you invoke using `npm` now reference your local scripts instead of referencing the `react-scripts` package. In turn, these scripts use the files found in the `config` directory that was created for you when you ran eject. Here are the relevant Webpack configuration files found here:

- `webpack.config.dev.js`
- `webpack.config.prod.js`
- `webpackDevServer.config.js`

Remember, these files are copied over from the `react-scripts` package. Ejecting simply means that you now control everything that was once hidden. It's still set up the exact same way and will remain so until you change it.

For example, let's suppose that you've decided that you need hot module replacement for React in a way that persists component state. Now that you've ejected from `create-react-app`, you can configure the necessary parts that enable the `react-hot-loader` tool. Let's start by installing the dependency:

```
npm install react-hot-loader --save-dev
```

Next, let's update the `webpack.config.dev.js` file so that it uses `react-hot-loader`. This is something that would have been impossible to configure before we ejected. There are two sections that need to be updated:

1. First, find the following line in the `entry` section:

   ```
   require.resolve('react-dev-utils/webpackHotDevClient'),
   ```

2. Replace this with the following two lines:

   ```
   require.resolve('webpack-dev-server/client') + '?/',
   require.resolve('webpack/hot/dev-server'),
   ```

3. Next, you have to add `react-hot-loader` to the `module` section of the Webpack configuration. Find the following object:

   ```
   {
     test: /\.(js|jsx|mjs)$/,
     include: paths.appSrc,
     loader: require.resolve('babel-loader'),
     options: {
       cacheDirectory: true,
     },
   }
   ```

4. Replace it with the following:

```
{
  test: /\.(js|jsx|mjs)$/,
  include: paths.appSrc,
  use: [
    require.resolve('react-hot-loader/webpack'),
    {
      loader: require.resolve('babel-loader'),
      options: {
        cacheDirectory: true,
      },
    }
  ]
},
```

All you're doing here is changing the `loader` option to the `use` option so that you can pass an array of loaders. The `babel-loader` that you were using stays the same. But now you've added the `react-hot-loader/webpack` loader as well. Now this tool can detect when it needs to hot replace React components when their source changes.

That's all you have to change with your development Webpack configuration. Next, you'll have to change the way that your root React component is rendered. Here's what `index.js` used to look like:

```
import React from 'react';
import ReactDOM from 'react-dom';
import './index.css';
import App from './App';
import registerServiceWorker from './registerServiceWorker';

ReactDOM.render(<App />, document.getElementById('root'));
registerServiceWorker();
```

To enable hot component replacement, you can change `index.js` so that it looks like this:

```
import 'react-hot-loader/patch';
import React from 'react';
import ReactDOM from 'react-dom';
import { AppContainer } from 'react-hot-loader';

import './index.css';
import App from './App';
import registerServiceWorker from './registerServiceWorker';

const render = Component => {
  ReactDOM.render(
```

```
        <AppContainer>
          <Component />
        </AppContainer>,
        document.getElementById('root')
      )
    };

    render(App);

    if (module.hot) {
      module.hot.accept('./App', () => {
        render(App);
      });
    }

    registerServiceWorker();
```

Let's break down what you've just added:

1. The `import 'react-hot-loader/patch'` statement is necessary to bootstrap the `react-hot-loader` mechanism.
2. You've created a `render()` function that accepts a component to render. The component is wrapped with the `AppContainer` component from `react-hot-loader`, which handles some of the bookkeeping associated with hot loading.
3. The first call to `render(App)` renders the application.
4. The call to `module.hot.accept()` sets up a callback function that renders the `App` component when a new version of the component arrives.

Now your app is ready to receive hot React component updates. It was always able to receive updates when your source changed, but as discussed earlier in the chapter, these updates will wipe out any state in the component before the component is re-rendered. Now that `react-hot-loader` is in place, you get to keep any state in your components. Let's try it out.

Once you load up the UI, click on the button a few times to change its state. Then, change the `style` constant to make the font bold:

```
const style = {
  fontWeight: 'bold'
};
```

Once you save this file, you'll notice that the button component has been updated. More importantly, the state hasn't changed! If you clicked on the button twice, it should look like this now:

This was a simple example that involved only one button. But the setup that you've just created by ejecting from `create-react-app`, tweaking the development Webpack configuration, and changing the way the `App` component is rendered can support hot component loading with every component you create going forward.

Adding the `react-hot-loader` package to your project is just one example of the need to eject from `create-react-app` so that you can tweak the configuration. I would caution against changing what's absolutely necessary. Make sure that you have a specific goal in mind when you change the configuration that `create-react-app` gives you. In other words, don't undo all the work that `create-react-app` has done for you.

Summary

In this chapter, you learned how to start the development server for a project created with `create-react-app`. You then learned that the `react-scripts` package has its own Webpack configuration that it uses when it starts the development server for you. We went over the key areas of configuration that you shouldn't necessarily have to think about when you're trying to write an application.

Finally, you saw hot module reloading in action. Out of the box, `react-scripts` reloads the app for you when you make source changes. This results in a page refresh, which is good enough to get started. We then looked at the potential challenges of developing components using this approach because it wipes out any state that the component had before it was updated. So you ejected from `create-react-app` and customized the Webpack configuration for your project to support hot component reloading that will preserve the state.

In the following chapter, you'll work with tooling to support unit tests in your React application.

4
Optimizing Test-Driven React Development

Perhaps, one of the most important tools in the React ecosystem is Jest—a test runner and unit test library for testing your React components. Jest was designed to overcome challenges faced with other test frameworks like Jasmine, and was created with React development in mind. With powerful testing tools like Jest, you're better equipped to let your unit tests influence the design of your React components. In this chapter, you'll learn:

- The overarching design philosophy of Jest and what this means for React developers
- Running Jest unit tests in a `create-react-app` environment and in a standalone React environment
- Writing effective unit tests and suites using the Jest API
- Running Jest unit tests in your code editor and integrating tests into your development server

The driving philosophy of Jest

In the previous chapter, you learned that the `create-react-app` tool was created to make developing React applications easier. It does so by eliminating upfront configuration—you go straight to building components. Jest was created with the same purpose in mind, eliminating the upfront boilerplate that you would typically have to create just to start writing tests. In addition to removing the initial unit test configuration factor, Jest has some other tricks up its sleeve. Let's go over some of the driving principles of testing with Jest.

Mock everything except the application code

The last thing you want to spend time on is testing someone else's code. Yet, sometimes you're forced to do exactly that. For example, let's say that you want to test a function that makes a `fetch()` call to some HTTP API. Another example: your React component uses some library to help set and manipulate its state.

In both of these examples, there's code that you didn't implement that's being run when your unit tests run. You definitely don't want to reach out to an external system over HTTP. You definitely don't want to make sure that the state of your component is being set correctly based on the output of functions from another library. For the code that we don't want to test, Jest provides a powerful mock system. But you need to draw a line somewhere—you can't mock every little thing.

Here's an illustration of a component and its dependencies:

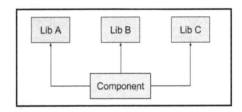

There are three libraries that this component requires in order to function. You probably don't want to unit test this component as is, because you would also be testing the functionality of three other libraries. The libraries that you don't want to run during unit testing can be mocked using Jest. You don't have to mock every library, and for some, mocking them may be more trouble than they're worth.

For example, let's say that **Lib C** in this scenario is a date library. Do you really need to mock it, or could you actually use the values it produces in component tests? A date library is pretty low level, so it's probably stable and it probably poses very little risk to the functioning of your unit test. On the other hand, the higher the level of the library and the more work that it does, the more problematic it is for your unit tests. Let's take a look at how this looks if you decided to use Jest to mock **Lib A** and **Lib B**:

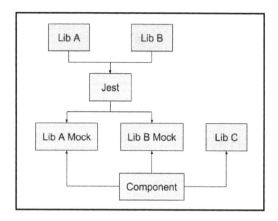

If you tell Jest that you want to mock implementations of **Lib A** and **Lib B**, it can use the actual modules and automatically create an object that your tests can use. So, with very little effort on your part, you can mock dependencies that pose challenges to testing your code.

Isolate tests and run in parallel

Jest makes it easy to isolate your unit tests in a sandboxed environment. In other words, side-effects from running one test cannot impact the results of other tests. Each time a test run completes, the global environment is automatically reset for the next. Since tests are standalone and their execution order doesn't matter, Jest runs tests in parallel. This means that even if you have hundreds of unit tests you can run them frequently without the fear of having to wait.

Here's an illustration of how Jest runs tests in parallel, in their own isolated environment:

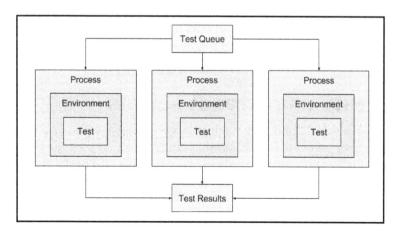

The best part is that Jest handles scaling processes up for you. For example, if you're just starting out and your project only has a handful of unit tests, Jest isn't going to spawn, for example, eight parallel processes. It will just run them in a single process. The key thing for you to remember is that unit tests are their own universe with no interference from other universes.

Tests should feel natural

Jest makes it easy to get started with running your tests, but what about writing tests? The API exposed by Jest makes it easy to write tests that don't have a lot of moving parts. The API documentation (`https://facebook.github.io/jest/docs/en/api.html`) is organized into sections that make it easy to find what you need. For example, if you're writing a test and you need to validate an expectation, you can find the functions that you need in the *Expect* section of the API docs. Or, you might need help configuring a mock function—the *Mock Functions* section of the API docs has everything you need on this topic.

Another area where Jest really stands out is when you need to test asynchronous code. This typically involves working with promises. The Jest API makes it easy to expect specific values from resolved or rejected promises without having to write a ton of async boilerplate. It's the little things like this that make writing unit tests for Jest feel like a natural extension of the actual application code.

Running tests

The Jest command-line tools are all you need to run your unit tests. There are a number of ways that the tool can be used. First, you'll learn how to invoke the test runner from a `create-react-app` environment and how to use the interactive watch mode options. Then, you'll learn how to run Jest in a standalone environment without the help of `create-react-app`.

Running tests using react-scripts

When you create your React application using `create-react-app`, you're ready to run tests right away. In fact, as part of the boilerplate code that's created for you, a unit test for the `App` component is created. This test is added so that Jest will find a test that it can run. It doesn't actually test anything meaningful in your application, so you'll probably delete it once more tests are added.

Additionally, `create-react-app` adds the appropriate script to your `package.json` file to run your tests. You can just run the following command in your Terminal:

```
npm test
```

This will actually invoke the `test` script from `react-scripts`. This will invoke Jest, which runs any tests that it finds. In this case, since you're working with a fresh project, it will only find the one test that `create-react-app` creates. Here's what the output of running this test looks like:

```
PASS   src/App.test.js
  ✓ renders without crashing (3ms)
Test Suites: 1 passed, 1 total
Tests:       1 passed, 1 total
Snapshots:   0 total
Time:        0.043s, estimated 1s
```

The test that was run lives in the `App.test.js` module—all Jest tests should have `test` somewhere in their filename. A good convention to follow is `ComponentName.test.js`. Then, you can see a list of tests that were run in this module, how long they took, and whether they passed or failed.

At the bottom, Jest prints out summary information of the run. This is often a good starting point because if all your tests are passing, you might not care about any other output. On the other hand when a test fails, the more information, the better.

The `test` script from `react-scripts` invokes Jest in watch mode. This means that you can choose which tests are actually run when files are changed. Here's what the menu looks like on the command line:

```
Watch Usage
 > Press a to run all tests.
 > Press p to filter by a filename regex pattern.
 > Press t to filter by a test name regex pattern.
 > Press q to quit watch mode.
 > Press Enter to trigger a test run.
```

When Jest is running in watch mode, the process doesn't exit as soon as all tests complete. Instead, it watches your test and component files for changes and runs tests when changes are detected. These options allow you to fine-tune which tests are run when changes take place. The p and t options are only useful if you have thousands of tests and many of them are failing. These options are useful to drill down and find the offending component as it's developed.

By default, when a change is detected by Jest, only associated tests are run. For example, changing the test or the component will result in the test being run again. With `npm test` running in your Terminal, let's open up `App.test.js` and make a small change to the test:

```
it('renders without crashing', () => {
  const div = document.createElement('div');
  ReactDOM.render(<App />, div);
});
```

You can just change the name of the test so that it looks like the following, and then save the file:

```
it('renders the App component', () => {
  const div = document.createElement('div');
  ReactDOM.render(<App />, div);
});
```

Now, take a look at your Terminal where you left Jest running in watch mode:

```
PASS  src/App.test.js
  ✓ renders the App component (4ms)
```

Jest detected the change in your unit test and ran it, producing the updated console output. Now let's introduce a new component and a new test and see what happens. First, you'll implement a `Repeat` component that looks like the following:

```
export default ({ times, value }) =>
  new Array(parseInt(times, 10))
    .fill(value)
    .join(' ');
```

This component takes a `times` property, which is used to determine how many times to repeat the `value` property. Here's how the `Repeat` component is used by the `App` component:

```
import React, { Component } from 'react';
import logo from './logo.svg';
import './App.css';
import Repeat from './Repeat';

class App extends Component {
  render() {
    return (
      <div className="App">
        <header className="App-header">
          <img src={logo} className="App-logo" alt="logo" />
          <h1 className="App-title">Welcome to React</h1>
```

```
        </header>
        <p className="App-intro">
          <Repeat times="5" value="React!" />
        </p>
      </div>
    );
  }
}

export default App;
```

If you were to view this application, you would see the string React! rendered five times on the page. Your component works as expected, but let's make sure that we add a unit test before committing your new component. Create a Repeat.test.js file that looks like this:

```
import React from 'react';
import ReactDOM from 'react-dom';
import Repeat from './Repeat';

it('renders the Repeat component', () => {
  const div = document.createElement('div');
  ReactDOM.render(<Repeat times="5" value="test" />, div);
});
```

This is actually the same unit test used for the App component. It doesn't test much other than that the component can render without triggering some sort of error. Now Jest has two component tests to run: one for App and the other one for Repeat. If you look at the console output for Jest, you'll see that both tests are run:

```
PASS   src/App.test.js
PASS   src/Repeat.test.js
Test Suites: 2 passed, 2 total
Tests:       2 passed, 2 total
Snapshots:   0 total
Time:        0.174s, estimated 1s
Ran all test suites related to changed files.
```

Pay attention to the last line in this output. The default watch mode of Jest is to look for files that haven't been committed to source control and that have been saved. By ignoring components and tests that have been committed, you know that they haven't changed, so running those tests would be pointless. Let's try changing the Repeat component and see what happens (you don't actually have to change anything, just saving the file is enough to trigger Jest):

```
PASS   src/App.test.js
PASS   src/Repeat.test.js
```

Why is the App test running? It's committed and hasn't been changed. The issue is that since App depends on Repeat, changes to the Repeat component could cause App tests to fail.

Let's introduce another component and test, except that this time we won't introduce any dependencies importing the new component. Create a Text.js file and save it with the following component implementation:

```
export default ({ children }) => children;
```

This Text component will just render whatever child element or text that is passed to it. It's a contrived component, but that doesn't matter. Now let's write a test that will verify that the component returns the value as expected:

```
import Text from './text';

it('returns the correct text', () => {
  const children = 'test';
  expect(Text({ children })).toEqual(children);
});
```

The toEqual() assertion passes when the value returned by Text() is equal to the children value. When you save this test, take a look at the Jest console output:

```
PASS   src/Text.test.js
 ✓ returns the correct text (1ms)
Test Suites: 1 passed, 1 total
Tests:       1 passed, 1 total
```

Now that you have a test that doesn't have any dependencies, Jest will run it on its own. The other two tests are checked into Git, so it knows that these tests do not need to run. You would never commit something that doesn't pass a unit test, right?

Let's make this test fail now and see what happens. Change the `Test` component so that it looks like this:

```
export default ({ children }) => 1;
```

This will fail the test because it is expecting the component function to return the value passed to the `children` property. Now if you go back to the Jest console, the output should look like this:

```
FAIL  src/Text.test.js
 ● returns the correct text
   expect(received).toEqual(expected)
   Expected value to equal:
     "test"
   Received:
     1
   Difference:
     Comparing two different types of values. Expected string but
     received number.
```

The test failed, as you knew it would. What's interesting is that once again, this was the only test that was run because nothing else has changed according to Git. The benefit to you is that once you have hundreds of tests, you don't need to wait for all of them to run before a failing test for the component that you're currently working can run.

Running tests using standalone Jest

The `test` script from `react-scripts` that you just learned about in the previous section is a great tool to have running in the background while you're building your application. It gives you immediate feedback as you implement components and unit tests.

Other times, you just want to run all tests and have the process exit as soon as the result output is printed. For example, if you're integrating Jest output into a continuous integration process or if you just want to see test results run once, you can run Jest directly.

Let's try running Jest on its own. Make sure that you're in your project directory still and that you've stopped the `npm test` script from running. Now just run:

```
jest
```

Rather than running Jest in watch mode, this command simply attempts to run all of your tests, prints the result output, and then exits. However, there seems to be a problem with this approach. Running Jest like this results in errors:

```
FAIL   src/Repeat.test.js
  ● Test suite failed to run
    04/my-react-app/src/Repeat.test.js: Unexpected token (7:18)
       5 |  it('renders the Repeat component', () => {
       6 |    const div = document.createElement('div');
    >  7 |    ReactDOM.render(<Repeat times="5" value="test"...
         |                    ^
       8 |  });
```

This is because the `test` script from `react-scripts` sets up a lot of things for us, including all of the Jest configuration necessary to parse and execute JSX. Given that we have this tool available to us, let's just use it rather than go through the headache of trying to configure Jest from scratch. Remember, your goal is to run Jest once—not in watch mode.

It turns out that the `test` script from `react-scripts` is ready to handle continuous integration environments. If it finds a `CI` environment variable, it won't run Jest in watch mode. Let's try this out by exporting this variable:

```
export CI=1
```

Now when you run `npm test`, everything works as expected. The process exits when everything is finished:

```
PASS   src/Text.test.js
PASS   src/App.test.js
PASS   src/Repeat.test.js
Test Suites: 3 passed, 3 total
Tests:       3 passed, 3 total
Snapshots:   0 total
Time:        1.089s
Ran all test suites.
```

You can then unset this environment variable when you're done:

```
unset CI
```

Most of the time, you'll probably just use Jest in watch mode. But in case you need to quickly run your tests in a short-lived process, you can temporarily enter continuous integration mode.

Writing Jest tests

Now that you know how to run Jest, let's write some unit tests. We'll cover the basics as well as the more advanced features of Jest available for testing React apps. We'll start organizing your tests into suites and the basic assertions available in Jest. Then, you'll create your first mock module and work with asynchronous code. Lastly, we'll use Jest's snapshotting mechanism to help test React component output.

Organizing tests using suites

Suites are the main organizational unit of your tests. Suites aren't a Jest requirement—the test that `create-react-app` creates does not include a suite:

```
it('renders without crashing', () => {
  ...
});
```

The `it()` function declares a unit test that passes or fails. When you're just getting your project started and you only have a few tests, there's no need for suites. Once you have several tests, it's time to start thinking about organization. Think of a suite as a container that you can put your tests in. You can have several of these containers that organize your tests however you see fit. Typically, a suite corresponds to a source module. Here's how you declare suites:

```
describe('BasicSuite', () => {
  it('passes the first test', () => {
    // Assertions...
  });

  it('passes the second test', () => {
    // Assertions...
  });
});
```

The `describe()` function is used here to declare a suite called `BasicSuite`. Within the suite, we have several unit tests declared. Using `describe()`, you can organize your tests so that related tests are grouped together in the test result output.

However, your tests will grow unwieldy fast if suites are the only mechanism available to organize your tests. The reason is that you will typically have more than one test per class, method, or function located within a module. So you need a way to say which part of code the test actually belongs to. The good news is that you can nest calls to describe() to provide the necessary organization for your suite:

```
describe('NestedSuite', () => {
  describe('state', () => {
    it('handles the first state', () => {

    });

    it('handles the second state', () => {

    });
  });

  describe('props', () => {
    it('handles the first prop', () => {

    });
    it('handles the second prop', () => {

    });
  });

  describe('render()', () => {
    it('renders with state', () => {

    });

    it('renders with props', () => {

    });
  });
});
```

The outermost describe() call declares the test suite, which corresponds to some top-level unit of code, such as a module. The inner calls to describe() correspond to smaller code units, such as methods and functions. This way, you can easily write several unit tests for a given piece of code while avoiding confusion about what's actually being tested.

Let's take a look at some detailed output for the test suite that you've just created. To do so, run the following:

```
npm test -- --verbose
```

The first set of double dashes tells `npm` to pass any arguments that follow to the `test` script. Here's what you'll see:

```
PASS  src/NestedSuite.test.js
  NestedSuite
    state
      ✓ handles the first state (1ms)
      ✓ handles the second state
    props
      ✓ handles the first prop
      ✓ handles the second prop
    render()
      ✓ renders with state
      ✓ renders with props (1ms)
PASS  src/BasicSuite.test.js
  BasicSuite
    ✓ passes the first test
    ✓ passes the second test
```

Under `NestedSuite`, you can see that `state` is the code that's being tested and that two tests have passed. Same is the case with `props` and `render()`.

Basic assertions

Assertions in your unit tests are created using Jest's expectation API. These functions trigger unit test failures when the expectations of your code aren't met. The output of test failures when using this API shows you what was expected to happen in addition to what actually happened. This seriously cuts down the amount of time you spend chasing down values.

Basic equality

You can assert that two values are the same by using the `toBe()` expectation method:

```
describe('basic equality', () => {
  it('true is true', () => {
    expect(true).toBe(true);
    expect(true).not.toBe(false);
  });

  it('false is false', () => {
    expect(false).toBe(false);
    expect(false).not.toBe(true);
  });
```

```
        });
```

In the first test, you're expecting `true` to equal `true`. Then, you're negating this expectation in the next line using the `.not` property. If this were a real unit test, you wouldn't have to prove the opposite of an assertion that you've just made like this—I'm doing this to illustrate some of your options.

In the second test, we're performing the same assertions but with `false` as the expectation value. The `toBe()` method uses strict equality to compare its values.

Approximate equality

There are times where checking for the exact value of something in your code makes no difference and could be more work than is worthwhile. For example, you might only need to make sure that a value is present. You might also need to perform the inverse—to make sure that there is no value. Something versus nothing in JavaScript terminology is **truthy** versus **falsy**.

To check for truthy or falsy values in your Jest unit tests, you would use the `isTruthy()` or `isFalsy()` methods respectively:

```
    describe('approximate equality', () => {
      it('1 is truthy', () => {
        expect(1).toBeTruthy();
        expect(1).not.toBeFalsy();
      });

      it('\'\' is falsy', () => {
        expect('').toBeFalsy();
        expect('').not.toBeTruthy();
      });
    });
```

The value 1 isn't true, but it evaluates to `true` when used in the context of a Boolean comparison. Likewise, an empty string evaluates to `false`, so it's considered falsy.

Value equality

When working with objects and arrays, checking for equality can be painful. You typically can't use strict equality because you're comparing references, which are always different. If it's the values that you're trying to compare, you need to iterate over the object or collection and compare the values, keys, and indexes individually.

Since no one in their right mind wants to do all of this work to perform a simple test. Jest provides the `toEqual()` method, which compares object properties and array values for you:

```
describe('value equality', () => {
  it('objects are the same', () => {
    expect({
      one: 1,
      two: 2
    }).toEqual({
      one: 1,
      two: 2,
    });

    expect({
      one: 1,
      two: 2
    }).not.toBe({
      one: 1,
      two: 2
    });
  });

  it('arrays are the same', () => {
    expect([1, 2]).toEqual([1, 2]);
    expect([1, 2]).not.toBe([1, 2]);
  });
});
```

Every object and array in this example are unique references. Yet, the two objects and the two arrays are equal in terms of their properties and values. The `toEqual()` method checks for value equality. After this, I'm showing that `toBe()` is not what you want—this returns `false` because it's comparing references.

Values in collections

There are way more assertion methods available in Jest than I have room to cover in this book. I encourage you to take a look at the *Expect* section of the Jest API docs:
`https://facebook.github.io/jest/docs/en/expect.html`.

The last two assertion methods I want to go over with you are `toHaveProperty()` and `toContain()`. The former tests that an object has a given property while the latter checks that an array contains a given value:

```
describe('object properties and array values', () => {
  it('object has property value', () => {
    expect({
      one: 1,
      two: 2
    }).toHaveProperty('two', 2);

    expect({
      one: 1,
      two: 2
    }).not.toHaveProperty('two', 3);
  });
  it('array contains value', () => {
    expect([1, 2]).toContain(1);
    expect([1, 2]).not.toContain(3);
  });
});
```

The `toHaveProperty()` method is useful when you need to check if an object has a particular property value. The `toContain()` method is useful when you need to check if an array has a particular value.

Working with mocks

When you write unit tests, you're testing your own code. At least that's the idea. In reality, this is more difficult than it sounds because your code will inevitably use a library of some sort. This is code that you do not want to test. The problem with writing unit tests that call other libraries is that they often need to reach out to the network or the filesystem. You definitely don't want false positives as a result of side-effects from other libraries.

Jest provides a powerful mocking mechanism that's easy to use. You give Jest the path to a module that you want to mock, and it handles the rest. In some cases, you don't need to provide a mock implementation. In other cases, you need to handle parameters and return values in the same way as the original module.

Let's say you've created a `readFile()` function that looks as follows:

```
import fs from 'fs';

const readFile = path => new Promise((resolve, reject) => {
  fs.readFile(path, (err, data) => {
    if (err) {
      reject(err);
    } else {
      resolve(data);
    }
  });
});

export default readFile;
```

This function requires the `readFile()` function from the `fs` module. It returns a promise that is resolved when the callback function that's passed to `readFile()` is called, unless there's an error.

Now you would like to write a unit test for this function. You want to make assertions like:

- Does it call `fs.readFile()`?
- Does the returned promise resolve with the correct value?
- Does the returned promise reject when the callback passed to `fs.readFile()` receives an error?

You can perform all of these assertions without relying on the actual implementation of `fs.readFile()` by mocking it with Jest. You don't have to make any assumptions about external factors; you only care that your code works the way that you expect it to.

So let's take a shot at implementing some tests for this function that use a mocked `fs.readFile()` implementation:

```
import fs from 'fs';
import readFile from './readFile';

jest.mock('fs');

describe('readFile', () => {
  it('calls fs.readFile', (done) => {
    fs.readFile.mockReset();
    fs.readFile.mockImplementation((path, cb) => {
      cb(false);
    });
```

```
    readFile('file.txt')
      .then(() => {
        expect(fs.readFile).toHaveBeenCalled();
        done();
      });
  });

  it('resolves a value', (done) => {
    fs.readFile.mockReset();
    fs.readFile.mockImplementation((path, cb) => {
      cb(false, 'test');
    });

    readFile('file.txt')
      .then((data) => {
        expect(data).toBe('test');
        done();
      });
  });

  it('rejects on error', (done) => {
    fs.readFile.mockReset();
    fs.readFile.mockImplementation((path, cb) => {
      cb('failed');
    });

    readFile()
      .catch((err) => {
        expect(err).toBe('failed');
        done();
      });
  });
});
```

The mocked version of the `fs` module is created by calling `jest.mock('fs')`. Note that you actually import the real `fs` module before mocking it and that it's mocked before any tests actually use it. In each test, we're creating a custom implementation of `fs.readFile()`. By default, functions mocked by Jest won't actually do anything. Rarely will this suffice for testing most things. The beauty of mocks is that you control the outcome of the library that your code uses, and your test assertions make sure that your code handles everything accordingly.

You provide the implementation by passing it as a function to the `mockImplementation()` method. But before you do this, always make sure that you call `mockReset()` to clear any stored information about the mock, like how many times it was called. For example, the first test has the assertion `expect(fs.readFile).toHaveBeenCalled()`. You can pass a mock function to `expect()` and Jest provides methods that know how to work with them.

The same pattern can be followed for similar functions. Here's the counterpart to `readFile()`:

```
import fs from 'fs';

const writeFile = (path, data) => new Promise((resolve, reject) => {
  fs.writeFile(path, data, (err) => {
    if (err) {
      reject(err);
    } else {
      resolve();
    }
  });
});

export default writeFile;
```

There's two important differences between `readFile()` and `writeFile()`:

- The `writeFile()` function accepts a second parameter for the data to write to the file. This parameter is also passed to `fs.writeFile()`.
- The `writeFile()` function doesn't resolve a value whereas `readFile()` resolves the file data that's been read.

These two differences have implications for the mock implementations that you create. Let's take a look at them now:

```
import fs from 'fs';
import writeFile from './writeFile';

jest.mock('fs');

describe('writeFile', () => {
  it('calls fs.writeFile', (done) => {
    fs.writeFile.mockReset();
    fs.writeFile.mockImplementation((path, data, cb) => {
      cb(false);
    });
```

```
      writeFile('file.txt')
        .then(() => {
          expect(fs.writeFile).toHaveBeenCalled();
          done();
        });
    });

    it('resolves without a value', (done) => {
      fs.writeFile.mockReset();
      fs.writeFile.mockImplementation((path, data, cb) => {
        cb(false, 'test');
      });

      writeFile('file.txt', test)
        .then(() => {
          done();
        });
    });

    it('rejects on error', (done) => {
      fs.writeFile.mockReset();
      fs.writeFile.mockImplementation((path, data, cb) => {
        cb('failed');
      });
  writeFile()
        .catch((err) => {
          expect(err).toBe('failed');
          done();
        });
    });
  });
```

The `data` parameter needs to be part of the mock implementation now; otherwise, there'd be no way to access the `cb` parameter and call the callback.

In both the `readFile()` and `writeFile()` tests, you have to deal with asynchronicity. This is why we're performing assertions within a `then()` callback. The `done()` function that is passed in from `it()` is called when we're done with the test. If you forget to call `done()`, the test will hang and eventually timeout and fail.

Asynchronous assertions

Jest anticipates that you'll have asynchronous code to test. This is why it provides APIs to make this aspect of writing unit tests feel natural. In the previous section, we wrote tests that performed assertions within a then() callback and called done() when all of the asynchronous testing was completed. In this section, we're going to look at another approach.

Jest allows you to return promise expectations from your unit test functions and will handle them accordingly. Let's refactor the readFile() tests that you wrote in the previous section:

```
import fs from 'fs';
import readFile from './readFile';

jest.mock('fs');

describe('readFile', () => {
  it('calls fs.readFile', () => {
    fs.readFile.mockReset();
    fs.readFile.mockImplementation((path, cb) => {
      cb(false);
    });
return readFile('file.txt')
      .then(() => {
        expect(fs.readFile).toHaveBeenCalled();
      });
  });

  it('resolves a value', () => {
    fs.readFile.mockReset();
    fs.readFile.mockImplementation((path, cb) => {
      cb(false, 'test');
    });

    return expect(readFile('file.txt'))
      .resolves
      .toBe('test');
  });

  it('rejects on error', () => {
    fs.readFile.mockReset();
    fs.readFile.mockImplementation((path, cb) => {
      cb('failed');
    });
```

```
    return expect(readFile())
      .rejects
      .toBe('failed');
  });
});
```

Now the tests return promises. When a promise is returned, Jest will wait for it to resolve before the results of the test are captured. You can also pass `expect()` a promise and use the `resolves` and `rejects` objects to perform your assertions. This way, you don't have to rely on the `done()` function to indicate that the asynchronous portion of your test is complete.

The `rejects` object is particularly valuable here. It's important to make sure that functions reject as expected. But without `rejects`, it's impossible to do this. In the previous version of this test, if your code resolved for some reason when it was supposed to reject, there's no way to detect this. Now if this happens, using `rejects` causes the test to fail.

React component snapshots

React components render output. Naturally, you want part of your component unit tests to ensure that the correct output is created. One approach is to render the component to a JS-based DOM, and then to perform individual assertions on the rendered output. This would be a painful test writing experience to say the least.

Snapshot testing allows you to generate a *snapshot* of rendered component output. Then, each time your test runs, the output is compared to the snapshot. If something looks different, the test fails.

Let's modify the default test for the `App` component that `create-react-app` adds for you to make it use snapshot testing. Here's what the original test looked like:

```
import React from 'react';
import ReactDOM from 'react-dom';
import App from './App';

it('renders without crashing', () => {
  const div = document.createElement('div');
  ReactDOM.render(<App />, div);
});
```

This test isn't actually verifying anything about the content that's rendered—just that an error isn't thrown. If you were to make a change that resulted in something unexpected, you would never know about it. Here's the snapshotting version of the same test:

```
import React from 'react';
import renderer from 'react-test-renderer';
import App from './App';

it('renders without crashing', () => {
  const tree = renderer
    .create(<App />)
    .toJSON();

  expect(tree).toMatchSnapshot();
});
```

Before this test would run, I had to install the `react-test-renderer` package:

```
npm install react-test-renderer --save-dev
```

Maybe this will be added to `create-react-app` some day. In the meantime, you'll have to remember to install it. Then, your test can import the test renderer and use it to create a JSON tree. This is a representation of the rendered component content. Next, you expect the tree to match the snapshot that is created the first time this test runs, using the `toMatchSnapshot()` assertion.

This means that the first time the test is run, it will always pass because this is when the snapshot is first created. Snapshot files are artifacts that should be committed to your project's source control system, just like the unit test source itself. This way, other folks who work on the project will have a snapshot file to work with when they run your tests.

What's misleading about snapshot testing is that it gives the impression that you can't actually change components to produce different output. Well, this is in fact true—changing the output produced by components will result in failed snapshot tests. This isn't a bad thing, though, as it forces you to look at what your components are rendering with every change you make.

Let's change the `App` component so that it adds emphasis to the word `started`:

```
<p className="App-intro">
  To get <em>started</em>, edit <code>src/App.js</code> and save to
  reload.
</p>
```

Now if you run your test, you get a failure that looks something like this:

```
Received value does not match stored snapshot 1.
- Snapshot
+ Received
 @@ -16,11 +16,15 @@
    </h1>
    </header>
    <p
       className="App-intro"
    >
-      To get started, edit
+      To get
+      <em>
+         started
+      </em>
+      , edit
```

Wow! This is useful. A unified diff shows you exactly what changed with the component output. You can look at this output and decide that this is exactly the change that you expected to see, or that you've made a mistake and you need to go fix it. Once you're happy with the new output, you can update the stored snapshot by passing an argument to the `test` script:

```
npm test -- --updateSnapshot
```

This will update the stored snapshot before running your tests and any failed snapshot tests will now pass since they meet their output expectations:

```
PASS  src/App.test.js
  ✓ renders without crashing (12ms)
Snapshot Summary
 > 1 snapshot updated in 1 test suite.
 Test Suites: 1 passed, 1 total
 Tests:       1 passed, 1 total
 Snapshots:   1 updated, 1 total
 Time:        0.631s, estimated 1s
```

Jest tells you that a snapshot was updated before running any tests, the result of passing the `--updateSnapshot` argument.

Unit test coverage

Jest comes with built-in support for test coverage reporting. It's nice to have this included as part of your test framework because not all of them have this support. If you want to see what your test coverage looks like, simply pass the `--coverage` option when starting Jest as follows:

```
npm test -- --coverage
```

When you do this, tests are run as normal. Then, the coverage tool inside Jest will figure out how well your tests cover your source, and will produce a report that looks like this:

```
----------|---------|----------|---------|---------|-----------------|
File      |% Stmts  | % Branch | % Funcs | % Lines |Uncovered Lines  |
----------|---------|----------|---------|---------|-----------------|
All files |   2.17  |       0  |   6.25  |   4.55  |                 |
 App.js   |    100  |     100  |    100  |    100  |                 |
 index.js |      0  |       0  |      0  |      0  | 1,2,3,4,5,7,8   |
----------|---------|----------|---------|---------|-----------------|
```

If you want to bring your coverage numbers up, take a look at the `Uncovered Lines` column in the report. The other columns tell you what type of code is covered by tests: statements, branches, and functions.

Summary

In this chapter, you learned about Jest. You learned that the key driving principles of Jest are creating effective mocks, test isolation and parallel execution, and ease of use. You then learned that `react-scripts` makes running your unit tests even easier by providing some basic configuration to use with Jest.

When running Jest, you saw that watch mode is the default when running Jest via `react-scripts`. Watch mode is especially useful when you have lots of tests that don't need to run every time you make a source change—only relevant tests are executed.

Next, you performed some basic assertions in your unit tests. Then, you created a mock for the `fs` module and performed assertions on the mocked functions to ensure that they're being used as expected. You then evolved these tests to make use of the inherent asynchronous capabilities of Jest. Unit test coverage reporting is built into Jest, and you learned how to view this report by passing an additional argument.

In the next chapter, you'll learn how to create type-safe components using Flow.

5
Streamlining Development and Refactoring with Type-Safe React Components

The tool of focus in this chapter is Flow, a static type checker for JavaScript applications. The scope of Flow and what you can do with it is enormous, so I'll be introducing Flow in the context of a tool that's used to make React components better. In this chapter, you'll learn the following:

- The problems that are solved by introducing type-safety into your React application
- Enabling Flow in your React projects
- Using Flow to validate your React components
- Other ways to enhance React development using type-safety

What does type-safety solve?

Type-safety is no silver bullet. For example, I'm perfectly capable of writing a type-safe application that's riddled with bugs. It's the kind of bugs that just sort of stop happening after a type-checker is introduced that are interesting. So what types of things can you expect after introducing a tool like Flow? I'll share three factors that I've experienced while learning Flow. The *Type System* section in the Flow docs goes into much more detail on this topic, available at `https://flow.org/en/docs/lang/`.

Replacing guesswork with assurance

One of the nice features of a dynamically-typed language like JavaScript is that you can write code without having to think about types. Types are good and they do solve a lot of problems—the point I'm trying to make, believe it or not—but sometimes you need to be able to just write code without having to formally validate for correctness. In other words, sometimes guesswork is exactly what you need.

If I'm writing a function that I know takes an object as an argument, I can just assume that any object that's passed to my function will have the expected properties. This allows me to implement what I need to, without having to make sure that the correct types are passed as arguments. This will only work for so long, though. Because invariably, your code will get something unexpected passed to it as input. Once you have a complex application with many moving parts, type-safety can remove the guesswork.

Flow takes an interesting approach. Instead of compiling new JavaScript code based on types, it simply checks that the source is correct based on type annotations. These annotations are then removed from the source so that it can run. By using a type checker like Flow, you can be explicit about what each of your components is willing to accept as input, and how it iterates with the rest of the application by using type annotations.

Removing runtime checks

The solution to handling data with unknown types in dynamic languages such as JavaScript is to check values at runtime. Depending on the type of value, you might have to perform some alternate action to get the value that your code is expecting. For example, a common idiom in JavaScript is to make sure that a value is neither undefined or null. If it is, then we either throw an error or provide a default value.

When you perform runtime checks, it changes the way you think about your code. Once you start performing these checks, they inevitably evolve into more elaborate checks and more of them. This frame of mind really amounts to not trusting yourself or others to call code with the correct data. You think since it's likely that your function will be called with junk arguments, you need to be ready to handle anything that is thrown at your function.

On the other hand, embracing type-safety means that you don't have to rely on implementing custom solutions to defend against bad data. Let the type system handle this for you instead. You just need to think about what types your code needs to work with, and go from there. Think what does my code need, not how do I get what my code needs.

Obvious low-severity bugs

If you can use a type checker such as Flow to remove the insidious errors that creep up on you as a result of bad types, you're left with high-level application bugs. These bugs are obvious when they happen because the application is simply wrong. It produces the wrong output, it computes the wrong number, one of the screens doesn't load, and so on. You can more easily see and interact with these kinds of bugs. This makes them obvious, and when bugs are obvious, they're easier to track down and fix.

On the other hand, you have bugs that are subtly wrong. These can result from bad types. What makes these types of bugs particularly horrifying is that you don't even know something is wrong. Something with your application could be slightly off. Or it could be outright broken because part of your code is expecting an array, but it sort of works because it's getting another kind of iterable that works in one place but not in others.

If you had just used type annotations and checked your source with Flow, it would have told you that you're passing something that isn't an array. There's no room for these types of errors when types are statically checked. It turns out that these are usually the more difficult bugs to figure out.

Installing and initializing Flow

Before you can start implementing type-safe React components, you need to install and initialize Flow. I'll show you how this is done with a `create-react-app` environment, but the same steps can be followed for almost any React environment.

You can install Flow globally, but I would recommend installing it locally, along with all the other packages that your project depends on. Unless there's a good reason to install something globally, install it locally. This way, anyone installing your application can get every dependency by running `npm install`.

To install Flow locally, run the following command:

```
npm install flow-bin --save-dev
```

This will install the Flow executable locally to your project and will update your `package.json` so that Flow is installed as a dependency of your project. Now let's add a new command to `package.json` so that you can run the Flow type checker against your source code. Make the `scripts` section look like this:

```
"scripts": {
  "start": "react-scripts start",
```

```
    "build": "react-scripts build",
    "test": "react-scripts test --env=jsdom",
    "eject": "react-scripts eject",
    "flow": "flow"
},
```

Now you can run Flow by executing the following command in your Terminal:

```
npm run flow
```

This will run the `flow` script as expected, but Flow will complain about not being able to find a Flow configuration file:

```
Could not find a .flowconfig in . or any of its parent directories.
```

The easiest way to resolve this issue is to use the `flow init` command:

```
npm run flow init
```

This will create a `.flowconfig` file in your project directory. You don't need to worry about changing anything in this file right now; it's just that Flow expects it to be present. Now when you run `npm run flow`, you should get a message that indicates there are no errors:

```
Launching Flow server for 05/installing-and-initializing-flow
Spawned flow server (pid=46516)
No errors!
```

It turns out that none of your source files were actually checked. This is because by default, Flow only checks files that have the `// @flow` directive as their first line. Let's go ahead and add this line at the top of `App.js`:

```
// @flow
import React, { Component } from 'react';
import logo from './logo.svg';
import './App.css';

class App extends Component {
  render() {
    return (
      <div className="App">
        <header className="App-header">
          <img src={logo} className="App-logo" alt="logo" />
          <h1 className="App-title">Welcome to React</h1>
        </header>
        <p className="App-intro">
          To get started...
```

```
        </p>
      </div>
    );
  }
}

export default App;
```

Now that Flow is checking this module, we're getting an error:

```
6: class App extends Component {
                     ^^^^^^^^^ Component. Too few type arguments.
Expected at least 1
```

What does this mean? Flow attempts to provide an explanation on the next line of the error output:

```
Component<Props, State = void> {
         ^^^^^^^^^^^^ See type parameters of definition here.
```

Flow is complaining about the Component class that you're extending with App. This means that you need to provide at least one type argument to Component for props. Since App isn't actually using any props, this could just be an empty type for now:

```
// @flow
import React, { Component } from 'react';
import logo from './logo.svg';
import './App.css';

type Props = {};

class App extends Component<Props> {
  render() {
    return (
      <div className="App">
        <header className="App-header">
          <img src={logo} className="App-logo" alt="logo" />
          <h1 className="App-title">Welcome to React</h1>
        </header>
        <p className="App-intro">
          To get started...
        </p>
      </div>
    );
  }
}
export default App;
```

Now when you run Flow again, there aren't any errors in `App.js`! This means that you've successfully annotated your module with type information that Flow used to statically analyze your source to make sure everything is sound.

So how did Flow know what the `Component` class from React was expecting in terms of its generics? It turns out that React is itself Flow type-annotated, and this is how you get specific error messages when Flow detects a problem.

Next, let's add the `// @flow` directive to the top of `index.js`:

```
// @flow
import React from 'react';
import ReactDOM from 'react-dom';
import './index.css';
import App from './App';
import registerServiceWorker from './registerServiceWorker';

const root = document.getElementById('root');

ReactDOM.render(
  <App />,
  root
);

registerServiceWorker();
```

If you run `npm run flow` again, you'll see the following error:

```
Error: src/index.js:12
  12:     root
          ^^^^ null. This type is incompatible with the expected param
               type of Element
```

This is because the value of `root` comes from `document.getElementById('root')`. Since there's no DOM for this method to return an element, Flow detects a `null` value and complains. Since this is a legitimate concern (the `root` element might not be there) and we need path for Flow to follow when there's no element, you can add some logic to handle this case:

```
// @flow
import React from 'react';
import ReactDOM from 'react-dom';
import './index.css';
import App from './App';
import registerServiceWorker from './registerServiceWorker';
```

```
const root = document.getElementById('root');

if (!(root instanceof Element)) {
  throw 'Invalid root';
}

ReactDOM.render(
  <App />,
  root
);

registerServiceWorker();
```

Before calling `ReactDOM.render()`, you can manually check the type of `root` to make sure that it's what Flow expects to see. Now when you run `npm run flow`, there are no errors.

You're all set! You have Flow installed and configured locally, and you have the initial source from `create-react-app` passing the type check. You can now proceed to develop type-safe React components.

Validating component properties and state

React was designed with Flow static type-checking in mind. The most common use of Flow in React applications is to validate that component properties and state are being used correctly. You can also enforce the types of components that are allowed as children of another component.

Prior to Flow, React would rely on the prop-types mechanism to validate values passed to components. This is now a separate package from React and you can still use it today. Flow is a superior choice over prop-types because it performs checks statically whereas prop-types performs runtime validation. This means that your application doesn't need to run superfluous code during runtime.

Primitive property values

The most common types of values that are passed to components via props are primitive values—strings, numbers, and Booleans for example. Using Flow, you can declare your own type that says which primitive values are allowed for a given property.

Let's take a look at an example:

```
// @flow
import React from 'react';

type Props = {
  name: string,
  version: number
};

const Intro = ({ name, version }: Props) => (
  <p className="App-intro">
    <strong>{name}:</strong>{version}
  </p>
);

export default Intro;
```

This component renders the name and version of some app. These values are passed in through property values. For this component, let's say that you only want string values for the `name` property and number values for the `version` property. This module declares a new `Props` type, using the `type` keyword:

```
type Props = {
  name: string,
  version: number
};
```

This Flow syntax allows you to create new types that can then be used to type function arguments. In this case, you have a functional React component where the props are passed as the first argument. This is where you tell Flow that the props object should have a specific type:

```
({ name, version }: Props) => (...)
```

With this in place, Flow can figure out if there's any places where we're passing invalid prop types to this component! Even better, this is done statically, before anything runs in the browser. Before Flow, you would have to use the `prop-types` package to validate component props during runtime.

Let's put this component to use, and then we'll run Flow. Here's `App.js` using the `Intro` component:

```
// @flow
import React, { Component } from 'react';
import logo from './logo.svg';
```

```
import './App.css';
import Intro from './Intro';

type Props = {};

class App extends Component<Props> {
  render() {
    return (
      <div className="App">
        <header className="App-header">
          <img src={logo} className="App-logo" alt="logo" />
          <h1 className="App-title">Welcome to React</h1>
        </header>
        <Intro name="React" version={16} />
      </div>
    );
  }
}

export default App;
```

The property values that are passed to Intro meet the expectations of the Props type:

```
<Intro name="React" version={16} />
```

You can validate this by running npm run flow. You should see No errors! as the output. Let's see what happens if we change the type of these properties:

```
<Intro version="React" name={16} />
```

Now we're passing a string where a number is expected, and a number where a string is expected. If you run npm run flow again, you should see the following errors:

```
    Error: src/App.js:17
      17:          <Intro version="React" name={16} />
                   ^^^^^^^^^^^^^^^^^^^^^^^^^^^^^^^^^^^^ props of React element
`Intro`. This type is incompatible with
        9: const Intro = ({ name, version }: Props) => (
                                            ^^^^^ object type. See:
    src/Intro.js:9
        Property `name` is incompatible:
           17:          <Intro version="React" name={16} />
                                                     ^^ number. This type is
    incompatible with
            5:    name: string,
                  ^^^^^^ string. See: src/Intro.js:5
        Error: src/App.js:17
```

```
    17:             <Intro version="React" name={16} />
                    ^^^^^^^^^^^^^^^^^^^^^^^^^^^^^^^^^^^^ props of React element
`Intro`. This type is incompatible with

     9: const Intro = ({ name, version }: Props) => (
                                           ^^^^^ object type. See:
src/Intro.js:9
      Property `version` is incompatible:
         17:             <Intro version="React" name={16} />
                                ^^^^^^^ string. This type is
incompatible with
          6:     version: number
                          ^^^^^^ number. See: src/Intro.js:6
```

These two errors go to great lengths to show you what the problem is. It starts by showing you where the component property values were passed:

```
<Intro version="React" name={16} />
       ^^^^^^^^^^^^^^^^^^^^^^^^^^^^^^^^^^^^ props of React element
`Intro`.
```

Then, it shows you where the Props type is being used—to declare the type of the properties argument:

```
This type is incompatible with
     9: const Intro = ({ name, version }: Props) => (
                                          ^^^^^ object type. See:
src/Intro.js:9
```

Finally, it shows you what the exact problem with the type is:

```
Property `name` is incompatible:
     17:             <Intro version="React" name={16} />
                                                  ^^ number. This type is
incompatible with
      5:     name: string,
                  ^^^^^^ string. See: src/Intro.js:5
```

The Flow error messages try to give you as much information as possible, meaning less time spent by you, hunting down files.

Object property values

In the preceding section, you learned how to check for primitive property types. React components can also accept objects with primitive values—and other objects. If your component is expecting an object as a property value, you can use the same approach as you did for primitive values. The difference is how you structure your `Props` type declaration:

```
// @flow
import React from 'react';

type Props = {
  person: {
    name: string,
    age: number
  }
};

const Person = ({ person }: Props) => (
  <section>
    <h3>Person</h3>
    <p><strong>Name: </strong>{person.name}</p>
    <p><strong>Age: </strong>{person.age}</p>
  </section>
);

export default Person;
```

This component expects a `person` property which is an object. Further, it expects this object to have a `name` string property and a number `age` property. In fact, if you had other components that required a `person` property, you could break this type down into reusable parts:

```
type Person = {
  name: string,
  age: number
};

type Props = {
  person: Person
};
```

Now let's take a look at values being passed to this component as properties:

```
// @flow
import React, { Component } from 'react';
import logo from './logo.svg';
import './App.css';
import Person from './Person';

class App extends Component<{}> {
  render() {
    return (
      <div className="App">
        <header className="App-header">
          <img src={logo} className="App-logo" alt="logo" />
          <h1 className="App-title">Welcome to React</h1>
        </header>
        <Person person={{ name: 'Roger', age: 20 }} />
      </div>
    );
  }
}

export default App;
```

Instead of passing the `Person` component several property values, it's passed a single property value, an object that meets the type expectations of the `Props` type. If it doesn't, Flow will complain. Let's try removing a property from this object:

```
<Person person={{ name: 'Roger' }} />
```

Now when you run `npm run flow`, it complains about the missing property of the object passed to `person`:

```
    15:              <Person person={{ name: 'Roger' }} />
                     ^^^^^^^^^^^^^^^^^^^^^^^^^^^^^^^^^^^^^^^^ props of React
    element `Person`. This type is incompatible with
        11: const Person = ({ person }: Props) => (
                                         ^^^^^ object type. See:
    src/Person.js:11
        Property `person` is incompatible:
            15:              <Person person={{ name: 'Roger' }} />
                                     ^^^^^^^^^^^^^^^^^^^ object literal. This
    type is incompatible with
                                 v
            5:    person: {
            6:       name: string,
            7:       age: number
```

```
8:    }
          ^ object type. See: src/Person.js:5
      Property `age` is incompatible:
                          v
      5:    person: {
      6:      name: string,
      7:      age: number
      8:    }
          ^ property `age`. Property not found in. See:
src/Person.js:5
     15:            <Person person={{ name: 'Roger' }} />
                           ^^^^^^^^^^^^^^^^^^^^ object literal
```

No matter how exotic you get with property values, Flow can figure out if you're misusing them. Trying to accomplish the same thing at runtime using something like `prop-types` is cumbersome at best.

Validating component state

You can validate the properties of functional React components by typing the props argument that's passed to the component. Some of your components will have state and you can validate a component's state much the same as with properties. You can create a type that represents the state of your component, and pass this to `Component` as a type argument.

Let's take a look at a container component that has state that is used and manipulated by a child component:

```
// @flow
import React, { Component } from 'react';
import Child from './Child';

type State = {
  on: boolean
};

class Container extends Component<{}, State> {
  state = {
    on: false
  }

  toggle = () => {
    this.setState(state => ({
      on: !state.on
    }));
```

```
    }

    render() {
      return (
        <Child
          on={this.state.on}
          toggle={this.toggle}
        />);
    }
  }

  export default Container;
```

The `Child` component rendered by `Container` takes an on Boolean property and a `toggle` function. The `toggle()` method that is passed to `Child` will change the state of `Container`. This means that `Child` can call this function in order to change the state of its parent. At the top of the module, above the component class, there's a `State` type that's used to specify what values are allowed to be set as state. In this case, the state is just a simple on Boolean value:

```
type State = {
  on: boolean
};
```

This type is then passed as a type argument to `Component` when it's extended:

```
class Container extends Component<{}, State> {
  ...
}
```

By passing this type argument to `Component`, you can bow set component state however you want. For example, the `toggle()` method is called by the `Child` component to change the state of the `Container` component. If this call sets the state incorrectly, Flow will detect it and complain. Let's change the `toggle()` implementation so that it fails by setting the state to something that disagrees with Flow:

```
toggle = () => {
  this.setState(state => ({
    on: !state.on + 1
  }));
}
```

You'll get an error that looks like this:

```
Error: src/Container.js:16
  16:         on: !state.on + 1
                  ^^^^^^^^^^^^ number. This type is incompatible with
   6:     on: boolean
              ^^^^^^ boolean
```

Setting the state incorrectly on a component is easy to do during development, so having Flow tell you what you're doing wrong is a real time saver.

Function property values

It's perfectly normal to pass functions from one component to another as a property. You can use Flow to ensure that not only are functions passed to the component, but also that the correction type of function is passed.

Let's examine this idea by looking at a common pattern in React applications. Let's say that you have the following Articles component that renders Article components:

```javascript
// @flow
import React, { Component } from 'react';
import Article from './Article';

type Props = {};
type State = {
  summary: string,
  selected: number | null,
  articles: Array<{ title: string, summary: string}>
};

class Articles extends Component<Props, State> {
  state = {
    summary: '',
    selected: null,
    articles: [
      { title: 'First Title', summary: 'First article summary' },
      { title: 'Second Title', summary: 'Second article summary' },
      { title: 'Third Title', summary: 'Third article summary' }
    ]
  }
}
```

```
onClick = (selected: number) => () => {
  this.setState(prevState => ({
    selected,
    summary: prevState.articles[selected].summary
  }));
}

render() {
  const {
    summary,
    selected,
    articles
  } = this.state;

  return (
    <div>
      <strong>{summary}</strong>
      <ul>
        {articles.map((article, index) => (
          <li key={index}>
            <Article
              index={index}
              title={article.title}
              selected={selected === index}
              onClick={this.onClick}
            />
          </li>
        ))}
      </ul>
    </div>
  );
}
}

export default Articles;
```

The `Articles` component is a container component because it has state and it uses this state to render child `Article` components. It also defines an `onClick()` method that changes the `summary` state and the `selected` state. The idea is that the `Article` component needs access to this method so that it can trigger state changes. If you pay close attention to the `onClick()` method, you'll notice that it's actually returning a new event handler function. This is so that when the click event actually calls the returned function, it will have scoped access to the selected argument.

Now let's take a look at the `Article` component and see how Flow can help you make sure that you're getting the function you expect passed to your component:

```
// @flow
import React from 'react';

type Props = {
  title: string,
  index: number,
  selected: boolean,
  onClick: (index: number) => Function
};

const Article = ({
  title,
  index,
  selected,
  onClick
}: Props) => (
  <a href="#"
    onClick={onClick(index)}
    style={{ fontWeight: selected ? 'bold' : 'normal' }}
  >
    {title}
  </a>
);

export default Article;
```

The `onClick` handler of the `<a>` element that this component renders calls the `onClick()` function that was pass in as a property, expecting a new function in return. If you take a look at the `Props` type declaration, you can see that the `onClick` property expects a specific type of function:

```
type Props = {
  onClick: (index: number) => Function,
  ...
};
```

This tells Flow that this property must be a function that accepts a number argument and returns a new function. Passing this component an event handler function instead of a function that returns the event handler function is an easy mistake to make. Flow can easily spot this and make it easy for you to correct.

Enforcing child component types

In addition to validating the types of state and property values, Flow can also validate that your component is getting the right child components as well. The following sections will show you common scenarios where Flow can tell you when you're misusing a component by passing it the wrong children.

Parents with specific children types

You can tell Flow that a component should only work with specific types of child components. Let's say that you have a `Child` component, and this is the only type of component that should be allowed as a child of the component you're working on. Here's how you can tell Flow about this constraint:

```
// @flow
import * as React from 'react';
import Child from './Child';

type Props = {
  children: React.ChildrenArray<React.Element<Child>>,
};

const Parent = ({ children }: Props) => (
  <section>
    <h2>Parent</h2>
    {children}
  </section>
);

export default Parent;
```

Let's start with the first `import` statement:

```
import * as React from 'react';
```

The reason that you want to import the asterisk as `React` is because this will pull in all of the Flow type declarations available within React. In this example, you're using the `ChildrenArray` type to specify that the value is in fact a child of the component, and `Element` to specify that you need a React element. The type argument that's used in this example tells Flow that the `Child` component is the only type of component that's acceptable here.

This JSX will pass flow validation, given the child constraints:

```
<Parent>
  <Child />
  <Child />
</Parent>
```

There's no restriction on the number of `Child` components that are rendered as children of `Parent`, just as long as there's at least one.

Parents with one child

For some components, it makes no sense to have more than one child. For these cases, you would use the `React.Element` type instead of the `React.ChildrenArray` type:

```
// @flow
import * as React from 'react';
import Child from './Child';

type Props = {
  children: React.Element<Child>,
};

const ParentWithOneChild = ({ children }: Props) => (
  <section>
    <h2>Parent With One Child</h2>
    {children}
  </section>
);

export default ParentWithOneChild;
```

As with the example before this one, you can still specify the type of child component that is allowed. In this case, the child component is called `Child`, imported from `'./Child'`. Here's how you would pass this component a child component:

```
<ParentWithOneChild>
  <Child />
</ParentWithOneChild>
```

If you were to pass it multiple `Child` components, Flow would complain:

```
Property `children` is incompatible:
    24:            <ParentWithOneChild>
                   ^^^^^^^^^^^^^^^^^^^^ React children array. Inexact
type is incompatible with exact type
     6:     children: React.Element<Child>,
                      ^^^^^^^^^^^^^^^^^^^^ object type. See:
src/ParentWithOneChild.js:6
```

Once again, the Flow error message shows you exactly what is wrong with your code and where.

Parents with an optional child

Always requiring a child component isn't necessary and can actually cause headaches. For example, what if there is nothing to render because nothing was returned from the API? Here's an example of how to specify that a child is optional using Flow syntax:

```
// @flow
import * as React from 'react';
import Child from './Child';

type Props = {
  children?: React.Element<Child>,
};

const ParentWithOptionalChild = ({ children }: Props) => (
  <section>
    <h2>Parent With Optional Child</h2>
    {children}
  </section>
);

export default ParentWithOptionalChild;
```

This looks a lot like a React component that requires a specific type of element. The difference is with the question mark: `children?`. This means that either a child component of type `Child` may be passed, or no child at all.

Parents with primitive child values

It's common to render React components that take primitive values as children. In some cases, you might want to accept a string or a Boolean type. Here's how you would do this:

```
// @flow
import * as React from 'react';

type Props = {
  children?: React.ChildrenArray<string|boolean>,
};

const ParentWithStringOrNumberChild = ({ children }: Props) => (
  <section>
    <h2>Parent With String or Number Child</h2>
    {children}
  </section>
);

export default ParentWithStringOrNumberChild;
```

Once again, you can use the `React.ChildrenArray` type to specify that multiple child elements are allowed. To specify a specific child type, you pass it to `React.ChildrenArray` as a type argument—in this case a string and Boolean union. Now you can render this component with a string:

```
<ParentWithStringOrNumberChild>
  Child String
</ParentWithStringOrNumberChild>
```

Or with a Boolean:

```
<ParentWithStringOrNumberChild>
  {true}
</ParentWithStringOrNumberChild>
```

Or with both:

```
<ParentWithStringOrNumberChild>
  Child String
  {false}
</ParentWithStringOrNumberChild>
```

Validating event handler functions

React components use functions to respond to events. These are called **event handler functions**, and they're passed an event object as an argument when the React event system calls them. It can be useful to use Flow to explicitly type these event arguments to make sure that your event handler is getting the type of element that it expects.

For example, assume that you're working on a component that responds to clicks from an <a> element. Your event handler function also needs to interact with the clicked element, in order to get the href property. Using the Flow types exposed by React, you can ensure that the correct element type is indeed triggering the event that is causing your function to run:

```
// @flow
import * as React from 'react';
import { Component } from 'react';

class EventHandler extends Component<{}> {
  clickHandler = (e: SyntheticEvent<HTMLAnchorElement>): void => {
    e.preventDefault();
    console.log('clicked', e.currentTarget.href);
  }

  render() {
    return (
      <section>
        <a href="#page1" onClick={this.clickHandler}>
          First Link
        </a>
      </section>
    );
  }
}

export default EventHandler;
```

The clickHandler() function in this example is assigned as the onClick handler of an <a> element. Notice the type of the event argument: SyntheticEvent<HTMLAnchorElement>. Flow will use this to make sure that your code that uses the event is only accessing the appropriate properties of the event, and currentTarget of the event.

`currentTarget` is the element that triggered the event, and in this example, you've specified that it should be `HTMLAnchorElement`. Had you used another type, Flow would complain about you referencing the `href` property, because that doesn't exist in other HTML elements.

Bringing Flow into the development server

Wouldn't it be great if type-checking your React code were more tightly-integrated into the `create-react-app` development process? There's been talk of making this a reality in a future release of `create-react-app`. For now, you'll have to eject from `create-react-app` if you want this functionality for your project.

The goal of this approach is to have the development server run Flow for you whenever changes are detected. Then, you can see the Flow output in your dev server console output, and in the browser console.

Once you've ejected from `create-react-app` by running `npm eject`, you need to install the following Webpack plugin:

```
npm install flow-babel-webpack-plugin --save-dev
```

Then, you need to enable the plugin by editing `config/webpack.config.dev.js`. First, you need to include the plugin:

```
const FlowBabelWebpackPlugin = require('flow-babel-webpack-plugin');
```

Then, you need to add the plugin to the array in the `plugins` option. This array should look something like this afterward:

```
plugins: [
  new InterpolateHtmlPlugin(env.raw),
  new HtmlWebpackPlugin({
    inject: true,
    template: paths.appHtml,
  }),
  new webpack.NamedModulesPlugin(),
  new webpack.DefinePlugin(env.stringified),
  new webpack.HotModuleReplacementPlugin(),
  new CaseSensitivePathsPlugin(),
  new WatchMissingNodeModulesPlugin(paths.appNodeModules),
  new webpack.IgnorePlugin(/^\.\/locale$/, /moment$/),
  new FlowBabelWebpackPlugin()
],
```

That's all there is to it. Now when you start your dev server, Flow will automatically run and type-check your code as part of the Webpack build process. Let's add the `@flow` directive to the top of `App.js` and run `npm start`. Since the `App` component won't validate as a subclass of `Component`, you should get an error in the dev server console output:

```
Failed to compile.
Flow: Type Error
Error: src/App.js:6
    6: class App extends Component {
                        ^^^^^^^^^^ Component. Too few type arguments.
Expected at least 1
      26: declare class React$Component<Props, State = void> {
                                        ^^^^^^^^^^^^^ See type parameters of
definition here.
    Found 1 error
```

What I really like about this approach is that the dev server will still start, even if there's a Flow error. If you look at the app in your browser, you'll see the following:

```
Failed to compile

Flow: Type Error
Error: src/App.js:6
  6: class App extends Component {
                      ^^^^^^^^^ Component. Too few type arguments. Expected at least 1
  26: declare class React$Component<Props, State = void> {
                                    ^^^^^^^^^^^^ See type parameters of definition here.


Found 1 error
Please wait. Server is garbage collecting shared memory: -

This error occurred during the build time and cannot be dismissed.
```

This means that you don't even have to look at your dev server console during development to catch type errors! And since it's part of the development dev server, your code is rechecked by Flow every time you make a change. So let's fix the current error in `App.js` by passing it a property type argument (`<{}>`):

```
class App extends Component<{}> {
   ...
}
```

Once this change is made, save the file. Just like that, the error is gone and you're back in business.

Bringing Flow into your editor

One final option that we'll look at for validating your React code using Flow is integrating the process into your code editor. I'm using the popular Atom editor so I'll use this as an example, but there are likely options for integrating Flow with other editors.

To enable Flow capabilities in the Atom (`https://atom.io/`) editor, you'll need to install the `linter-flow` package:

Once installed, you'll need to change the executable path setting of `linter-flow`. By default, the plugin assumes that you have Flow installed globally, which, you probably don't. You have to tell the plugin to look in the local `node_modules` directory for the Flow executable:

You're all set. To verify that this is working as expected, open up `App.js` from a fresh `create-react-app` install and add the `@flow` directive at the top of the file. This should trigger an error from Flow and should be displayed within Atom:

The Linter will also highlight the problematic code that's causing Flow to complain as well:

```
5
6  • class App extends Component {
7      render() {
8        return (
```

With the in-editor approach to using Flow, you don't even have to save, let alone switch windows to have your code type-checked—all you have to do is write it.

Summary

In this chapter, you learned about why type-checking your React code matters. You also learned about Flow—the tool used to type-check React code. Type-checking is important for React applications because it removes the need to perform runtime checks of values in the majority of cases. This is because Flow is able to statically follow code paths and determine whether everything is being used as intended.

Then, you installed Flow locally to a React application and learned how to run it. Next, you learned the basics of validating property and state values of React components. Then you learned how to validate function types and how to enforce child React component types.

Flow can be used in `create-react-app` dev server, but you have to eject first. In future versions of `create-react-app`, there will likely be better integrated support for running Flow as part of the dev server. Another option is to install a Flow plugin in a code editor such as Atom, and have errors displayed right in front of your eyes as you write your code.

In the following chapter, you'll learn how to enforce a high quality level with your React code with the help of tools.

6
Enforcing Code Quality to Improve Maintainability

Wouldn't it be nice if a project's code were consistent and easy to read? The reason that this isn't often the case is because enforcing such a level of code quality is burdensome. When something is a burden when done manually, you introduce a tool.

The focus of this chapter is on using tools that assist with making sure that your React code quality is up to standards. Here's what you'll learn in this chapter:

- Installing and configuring ESLint
- Running ESLint on React source code
- Getting configuration help from Airbnb
- Linting JSX and React components
- Integrating ESLint with your code editor
- Customizing ESLint errors and warnings
- Formatting code automatically with Prettier

Installing and configuring ESLint

The first step to automating the quality of your React source code is installing and configuring the tool used to automate it—ESLint. When ESLint is installed, it installs an `eslint` command on your system. Like other packages that install commands, it's better to have them installed locally as part of the project, so that you don't have to rely on the command being available globally on the system.

To install ESLint in your project, run the following `npm` command:

```
npm install eslint --save-dev
```

Now that you have ESLint installed, you can create a new npm script that will run ESLint for you. Add the following to the `scripts` section of your `package.json` file:

```
"scripts": {
  ...
  "lint": "eslint"
},
```

You now have an `eslint` command that you can run within your project. Try it out:

```
npm run lint
```

Instead of linting any of your source files, you should see a usage message in your console:

```
eslint [options] file.js [file.js] [dir]
Basic configuration:
  -c, --config path::String      Use configuration from this file or
shareable config
    --no-eslintrc                Disable use of configuration from
.eslintrc
    --env [String]               Specify environments
    --ext [String]               Specify JavaScript file extensions -
default: .js
    --global [String]            Define global variables
    --parser String              Specify the parser to be used
    --parser-options Object      Specify parser options
  ...
```

As you can see, you have to tell the `eslint` command which files or directories you want to lint. To keep things simple, let's assume that all of our code is in the same directory as `package.json`. You can modify your `package.json` file as follows so that ESLint knows where to look for files:

```
"scripts": {
  ...
  "lint": "eslint ."
},
```

Did you notice the dot (.) added after `eslint`? This means the current directory on most systems. Go ahead and run `npm run lint` again. This time, you'll see a different output as ESLint is actually attempting to find source files to lint:

```
Oops! Something went wrong! :(

ESLint: 4.15.0.
ESLint couldn't find a configuration file. To set up a configuration file
for this project, please run:
    eslint --init
```

Okay, so let's do what it's telling us to do. We'll run `npm run lint -- --init` to create a configuration file. When you do this, you're presented with a number of options to choose from:

```
? How would you like to configure ESLint?
> Answer questions about your style
  Use a popular style guide
  Inspect your JavaScript file(s)
```

Let's go with the first option for now and answer some basic questions about the code you plan on writing. With the option selected, pressing *Enter* brings you to the first question:

```
? Are you using ECMAScript 6 features? (y/N)
```

Yes, you are.

```
? Are you using ES6 modules? (y/N)
```

Yes, you are.

```
? Where will your code run? (Press <space> to select, <a> to toggle all,
<i> to inverse selection)
>(*) Browser
  ( ) Node
```

Select `Browser`.

```
? Do you use CommonJS? (y/N)
```

Nope.

```
? Do you use JSX? (y/N)
```

Nope. We'll get into JSX later in this chapter.

```
? What style of indentation do you use? (Use arrow keys)
> Tabs
  Spaces
```

Use whatever you like here, because I'll inevitably be wrong.

```
? What quotes do you use for strings? (Use arrow keys)
> Double
  Single
```

Single. What are you, an animal?

```
? What line endings do you use? (Use arrow keys)
> Unix
  Windows
```

Unix is a safe bet here.

```
? Do you require semicolons? (Y/n)
```

This is a tricky one. Semicolons aren't a requirement in JavaScript source. There are times where they can help, while other times they're just added syntax for something that the JavaScript interpreter already understands. If you're unsure, require semicolons; you can always change your ESLint configuration later on:

```
? What format do you want your config file to be in? (Use arrow keys)
> JavaScript
  YAML
  JSON
```

Use whatever you're most comfortable with reading and editing. I'm going to stick with the default option of JavaScript:

```
Successfully created .eslintrc.js file
```

Hooray! Let's try running this again:

```
npm run lint
```

No output this time. This just means that ESLint didn't find any errors. Part of that has to do with the fact that there's no code in the project yet, but you now have a known working starting point. Let's take a quick look at the .eslintrc.js file that was created for you:

```
module.exports = {
    "env": {
        "browser": true,
        "es6": true
    },
    "extends": "eslint:recommended",
    "parserOptions": {
        "sourceType": "module"
```

```
        },
        "rules": {
            "indent": [
                "error",
                4
            ],
            "linebreak-style": [
                "error",
                "unix"
            ],
            "quotes": [
                "error",
                "single"
            ],
            "semi": [
                "error",
                "always"
            ]
        }
    };
```

Since you've answered the questions required to create this file, you don't need to change anything yet. When you do, this is the file to edit. When you're just learning ESLint, typing out a configuration file like this can be off putting. In time, when you decide that your code quality standards need tweaking, the ESLint rules reference (https://eslint.org/docs/rules/) is a great resource.

As the final step to setting up and configuring ESLint for your project, let's introduce some source code to lint. Create an index.js file if it doesn't already exist, and add the following function:

```
export const myFunc = () => 'myFunc';
```

Don't worry about running this function, linting does not serve the same purpose as testing or types. Instead, linting provides the developer with easy-to-miss hints about something they've done wrong from a code-quality perspective. Correctness is different from code quality. This means that you have a wide variable of tweakable options with ESLint that tell it how to evaluate your code.

Now, back to the function you've just added. You can verify that this function is okay by running npm run lint again. Sure enough, the function is good according to the rules that you've configured in .eslintrc.js. Now, try removing the semicolon from the function so that it looks like this:

```
export const myFunc = () => 'myFunc'
```

This time, you get an error from ESLint:

```
index.js
  1:37  error  Missing semicolon  semi
X 1 problem (1 error, 0 warnings)
```

This is the exact kind of output you need. It gives you the name of the source file, the location of the error/warning in the file, and describes the actual problem that was found.

Let's try one more. Go ahead and restore the semicolon that you deleted. Now, delete the `export` statement so that your function definition looks as follows:

```
const myFunc = () => 'myFunc';
```

Now you get a different error when this code is linted:

```
index.js
  1:7  error  'myFunc' is assigned a value but never used  no-unused-vars
X 1 problem (1 error, 0 warnings)
```

Because you've removed the `export` keyword, the module is just a function assigned to `myFunc`. It's never used, and ESLint was able to tell you about it.

Building on Airbnb standards

Organizations that have large JavaScript code bases have invested heavily in code quality tools. This includes investments in configuring tools like ESLint. The great part about using a standard set of configuration values for enforcing code quality is that you don't have any discrepancies between developers due to a slight configuration difference.

ESLint allows you to install and use npm packages as configuration settings to use and extend. A popular choice is the Airbnb standard. Let's use the ESLint `init` tool again to get started with Airbnb JavaScript code quality standards. First, run the `init` tool again:

```
npm run lint -- --init
```

The first question asks you how you want to configure ESLint. Instead of answering questions, you can choose a guide:

```
? How would you like to configure ESLint?
  Answer questions about your style
> Use a popular style guide
  Inspect your JavaScript file(s)
```

The next question lets you choose which guide to follow. You want Airbnb's guide:

```
? Which style guide do you want to follow?
  Google
› Airbnb
  Standard
```

Now, ESLint will install the necessary npm packages for using Airbnb's ESLint configuration settings:

```
Checking peerDependencies of eslint-config-airbnb-base@latest
Installing eslint-config-airbnb-base@latest, eslint-plugin-import@^2.7.0

+ eslint-plugin-import@2.8.0
+ eslint-config-airbnb-base@12.1.0
```

Let's see what the .eslintrc.js file that ESLint created looks like:

```
module.exports = {
  "extends": "airbnb-base"
};
```

As you can see, there's very little to this file now because everything is handled by the airbnb-base npm package. Your .eslintrc.js is simply extending it. So let's see some of these Airbnb rules in action. Add the following code to index.js:

```
const maybe = v => v ? v : 'default';

console.log(maybe('yes'));
// -> yes
console.log(maybe());
// -> default
```

The maybe() function returns the argument if it's truthy; otherwise, it returns the string default. Then, maybe() is called with a string value, and no value at all. The comments indicate the output of these two function calls. Feel free to run this code to make sure that it works as advertised.

After you do that, let's see what Airbnb thinks about your code:

```
npm run lint
```

And here's the output:

```
index.js
  1:15  error    Arrow function used ambiguously with a conditional
expression    no-confusing-arrow
```

```
   1:24   error     Unnecessary use of conditional expression for default
assignment   no-unneeded-ternary
   3:1    warning   Unexpected console statement
no-console
   5:1    warning   Unexpected console statement
no-console
X 4 problems (2 errors, 2 warnings)
```

Four problems! Ouch. Let's walk through each of them and see what can be done. The first error is `no-confusing-arrow`, which says that an arrow function was used ambiguously with a comparison operator. You can go look at the specifics of each error (`https://eslint.org/docs/rules/`) where you'll find detailed explanations and examples.

The next error, `no-unneeded-ternary`, is closely related to the first error. It states that we can use a simpler expression than a ternary, which should help with the readability of your code. So let's try it out. The `maybe()` function is supposed to return either the argument or some default value if the argument is falsy. Instead of a ternary operator, let's try using a logical OR (||):

```
const maybe = (v = 'default') => v;
```

There's a slight improvement in readability here, definitely less syntax. What's more important about the minor improvement itself is the fact that every developer working on this code base will make the same minor improvement. Let's see what `npm run lint` says now:

```
index.js
   6:1   warning   Unexpected console statement   no-console
   8:1   warning   Unexpected console statement   no-console
X 2 problems (0 errors, 2 warnings)
```

Awesome! You're down to two warnings. But these are just complaining about your `console.log()` calls. Clearly, the Airbnb ESLint rules don't like that, but you do. Since you're just using the Airbnb rule settings as a starting point by extending them, you can also turn them off. In your case, the `no-console` rule is serving no purpose since you clearly rely on it. To do so, edit your `.eslintrc.js` file to look like this:

```
module.exports = {
  "extends": "airbnb-base",
  "rules": {
    "no-console": 0
  }
};
```

After the `extends` section of the ESLint configuration, you can add a `rules` section where you can turn off specific rules that are defined by `airbnb-base`. In this example, setting `no-console` to 0 tells ESLint that it shouldn't report these warnings. Let's run `npm run lint` one more time to see if this has fixed everything.

Sure enough, there are no more errors to report!

Adding React plugins to ESLint

Let's assume that you want to use the Airbnb set of ESLint rules after having tried it out and liking it. Let's also assume that you want to lint your React component code as well. During the ESLint `init` process, you've answered `No` to the question that asks whether or not your project uses React. This time, let's say `Yes`. So, once again, run the ESLint `init` process:

```
npm run lint -- --init
```

And once again, you want to use the Airbnb lint rules:

```
? Which style guide do you want to follow?
  Google
> Airbnb
  Standard
```

When it asks if you use React, say `Yes`:

```
? Do you use React? (y/N) y
```

You'll notice that a couple of extra packages are installed:

```
+ eslint-plugin-react@7.5.1
+ eslint-plugin-jsx-a11y@6.0.3
```

Now let's write some React code so that we can lint it. Add the following component to `MyComponent.js`:

```
import React, { Component } from 'react';

class MyComponent extends Component {
  render() {
    return (
      <section>
        <h1>My Component</h1>
      </section>
    );
```

```
    }
  }

  export default MyComponent;
```

And here is how this component is rendered:

```
import React from 'react';
import ReactDOM from 'react-dom';
import MyComponent from './MyComponent';

const root = document.getElementById('root');

ReactDOM.render(
  <MyComponent />,
  root
);
```

You don't need to worry about running this React app in your browser; this is just so that you can make sure that ESLint is able to parse JSX and lint it. Let's try running ESLint now:

```
npm run lint
```

Here are the errors this source code generates when linted:

```
index.js
  5:14  error  'document' is not defined                        no-undef
  8:3   error  JSX not allowed in files with extension '.js'     react/jsx-
filename-extension
  9:7   error  Missing trailing comma                            comma-dangle

MyComponent.js
  3:1   error  Component should be written as a pure function    react/prefer-
stateless-function
  6:7   error  JSX not allowed in files with extension '.js'     react/jsx-
filename-extension
```

You have errors in both source files to deal with. Let's walk through each of these errors now.

The first error from `index.js` is `no-undef` and it's referring to a `document` identifier that doesn't exist. The thing is, you know that `document` is an identifier that exists globally in a browser environment. ESLint doesn't know that this global identifier is defined, so we have to tell it about the value in `.eslintrc.js`:

```
module.exports = {
  "extends": "airbnb",
```

```
    "globals": {
      "document": true
    }
};
```

In the `globals` section of the ESLint configuration, you can list the names of global identifiers that ESLint should recognize. The value should be `true` if the identifier is in fact globally available to source code that references it. This way, ESLint knows not to complain about something that is recognized as a global identifier in a browser environment.

The problem with adding globals for identifiers that exist in a specific environment, like a web browser, is that there are a lot of them. You wouldn't want to have to maintain a list like this just so that ESLint passes your source code. Thankfully, ESLint has a solution for this. Rather than specifying `globals`, you can specify the environment that your code will be running in:

```
module.exports = {
  "extends": "airbnb",
  "env": {
    "browser": true
  }
};
```

With the `browser` environment specified as `true`, ESLint knows about all of the browser globals and will not complain when it finds them in your code. Further, you can specify multiple environments, as it's common to have code that runs both in the browser and in Node.js. Or even if you don't share code between environments, you might want to lint a project that has both client and server code. In either case, here's what multiple ESLint environments:

```
module.exports = {
  "extends": "airbnb",
  "env": {
    "browser": true,
    "node": true
  }
};
```

The next error to fix is `react/jsx-filename-extension`. This rule comes from the `eslint-plugin-react` package that was installed when you initialized your ESLint configuration. The rule expects you to name files that contain JSX syntax using a different extension. Let's assume that you don't want to bother with this (not that I would blame you, that's a lot of effort to maintain two file extensions for almost the same type of file contents). Let's disable this rule for now.

Here's the updated ESLint configuration:

```
module.exports = {
  "extends": "airbnb",
  "env": {
    "browser": true,
    "node": true
  },
  "rules": {
    "react/jsx-filename-extension": 0
  }
};
```

The `react/jsx-filename-extension` rule is ignored by setting its value to 0 in the `rules` section of the configuration. Go ahead and run `npm run lint` again. We're down to two errors now.

The `comma-dangle` rule is opinionated to be sure, but it's an interesting idea. Let's zoom in on the offending code that triggered this error:

```
ReactDOM.render(
  <MyComponent />,
  root
);
```

ESLint is complaining that there's no trailing comma after the `root` argument. The idea is that when trailing commas are added:

- It's easier to add items later on because the comma is already there
- It leads to cleaner diffs when you commit code because adding or removing items only requires changing one line instead of two

Let's assume that this makes sense and you decide to keep this rule (I like it), here's what the fixed code looks like:

```
ReactDOM.render(
  <MyComponent />,
  root,
);
```

Now let's run `npm run lint` again. One error left! It's another React-specific error: `react/prefer-stateless-function`. Let's take another look at your React component that triggered this error:

```
import React, { Component } from 'react';
```

```
class MyComponent extends Component {

  render() {
    return (
      <section>
        <h1>My Component</h1>
      </section>
    );
  }
}

export default MyComponent;
```

ESLint, with the help of `eslint-plugin-react`, is telling you that this component should be implemented as a function instead of a class. It says this because it was able to detect that `MyComponent` doesn't have any state and it doesn't have any life cycle methods. So if it were implemented as a function, it:

- Would no longer depend on the `Component` class
- Would be a simple function with far less syntax than a class
- Would be obvious that there are no side-effects with this component

With these benefits in mind, let's go ahead and refactor `MyComponent` into a pure function as the ESLint error suggests:

```
import React, { Component } from 'react';

const MyComponent = () => (
  <section>
    <h1>My Component</h1>
  </section>
);

export default MyComponent;
```

And when you run `npm run lint`, you get:

```
MyComponent.js
  1:17  error  'Component' is defined but never used  no-unused vars
```

Woops, you've introduced a new error in the process of fixing another. No big deal, this is why you lint your code, to find things that are easy to miss. In this case, it's the `no-unused-vars` error because we forgot to take out the `Component` import. Here's the fixed version:

```
import React from 'react';
const MyComponent = () => (
```

```
    <section>
      <h1>My Component</h1>
    </section>
);

export default MyComponent;
```

And you're done, no more errors! With the help of `eslint-config-airbnb` and `eslint-plugin-react`, you were able to produce code that any other React developer will have an easy time reading because chances are they're using the exact same code quality standards.

Using ESLint with create-react-app

Everything you've seen so far in this chapter, you've had to set up and configure yourself. Not that getting ESLint up and running is particularly difficult or anything, but `create-react-app` abstracts this away completely. Remember, the idea with `create-react-app` is start writing component code as soon as possible, without having to think about configuring things like linters.

To see this in action, let's create a new app using `create-react-app`:

```
create-react-app my-new-app
```

Then, start the app as soon as it's created:

```
npm start
```

Now let's get ESLint to complain about something. Open up `App.js` in your editor—it should look something like this:

```
import React, { Component } from 'react';
import logo from './logo.svg';
import './App.css';

class App extends Component {
  render() {
    return (
      <div className="App">
        <header className="App-header">
          <img src={logo} className="App-logo" alt="logo" />
          <h1 className="App-title">Welcome to React</h1>
        </header>
        <p className="App-intro">
          To get started, edit <code>src/App.js</code> and save to reload.
```

```
      </p>
    </div>
  );
 }
}
```

```
export default App;
```

ESLint thinks this is fine, so let's delete the `Component` import so that `App.js` looks like this now:

```
import React from 'react';
import logo from './logo.svg';
import './App.css';

class App extends Component {
  render() {
    return (
      <div className="App">
        <header className="App-header">
          <img src={logo} className="App-logo" alt="logo" />
          <h1 className="App-title">Welcome to React</h1>
        </header>
        <p className="App-intro">
          To get started, edit <code>src/App.js</code> and save to reload.
        </p>
      </div>
    );
  }
}

export default App;
```

Your `App` class is now trying to extend `Component`, which doesn't exist. Once you save the file, ESLint will be invoked as it's integrated with the development server as a Webpack plugin. In the dev server console, you should see the following:

```
Failed to compile.
./src/App.js
Line 5:  'Component' is not defined  no-undef
```

As expected, ESLint detects the issue for you. What's nice about having ESLint integrated with the development server is that you don't have to remember to invoke the `npm run lint` command. If ESLint doesn't pass, the entire build fails.

Not only are you notified about the failed build in the dev server console, but you're also notified directly in the browser:

```
Failed to compile

./src/App.js
  Line 5:  'Component' is not defined  no-undef

Search for the keywords to learn more about each error.

This error occurred during the build time and cannot be dismissed.
```

This means that even if you forget to look at the server console, it's hard to miss the one that replaces your entire UI. If you undo that change that intentionally broke ESLint (add the `Component` import back), your UI shows up once again as soon as you save `App.js`.

Using ESLint in a code editor

If you want to take linting your `create-react-app` code a step further, you can. If you're in the middle of writing component code, the last thing you want to have to do is switch to either the console or the browser window, just to see if what you're writing is good enough. For some people, a better development experience is to see the lint errors as they happen, in their editors.

Let's take a look at how to do this with Atom. First, you need to install the `linter-eslint` plugin:

Now when you open JavaScript source files in Atom, this plugin will lint them for you and display errors and warnings inline. The only challenge is that `create-react-app` doesn't actually create an `.eslintrc.js` file for you. This is because the nature of `create-react-app` is to hide all configuration from you by default.

However, ESLint is still configured by `create-react-app`. This is how your source is linted when you start the development server. The problem is that you might want to use this configuration in your editor linter. There is a package installed by `create-react-app` called `eslint-config-react-app` that contains the ESLint configuration used by the development server. You can use this in your own project so that your editor linter is configured the same as anything that is output in the browser or the console. This is really important, the last thing you want is to have your editor telling you one thing about your code while you don't see any issues in the browser.

If you open up `App.js` in Atom, you shouldn't see any lint errors because:

- There aren't any
- The `linter-eslint` Atom plugin isn't running because it didn't find any configuration

Here's what the file looks like when there are no errors:

```
                   App.js
 1   import React from 'react';
 2   import logo from './logo.svg';
 3   import './App.css';
 4
 5   class App extends Component {
 6     render() {
 7       return (
 8         <div className="App">
 9           <header className="App-header">
10             <img src={logo} className="App-logo" alt="logo" />
11             <h1 className="App-title">Welcome to React</h1>
12           </header>
13           <p className="App-intro">
14             To get started, edit <code>src/App.js</code> and save to reload.
15           </p>
16         </div>
17       );
18     }
19   }
20
21   export default App;
```

All you have to do is add ESLint configuration that extends the `eslint config-react-app` configuration. In the root of your project, create the following `.eslintrc.js` file:

```
module.exports = {
  "extends": "eslint-config-react-app"
};
```

Now the Atom `linter-eslint` plugin will attempt to lint your open source files on-the-fly. Further, it will use the exact same configuration as your `create-react-app` dev server. Let's try deleting the `Component` import again. Things look a little different in your editor now:

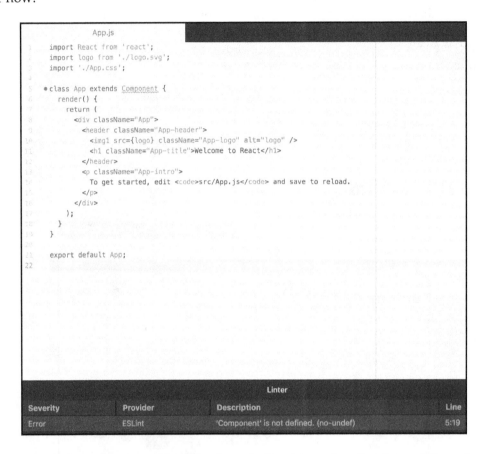

As you can see, the `Component` identifier is underlined in red so that this portion of your code stands out. Underneath your source, there is a pane that shows a list of every linter error found, along with more details about each error. If you were to run `npm start`, you would see the exact same error in the dev server console and in the browser because Atom is using the same ESLint configuration as `create-react-app`.

Now let's get rid of this error. Go to the following code line:

```
import React from 'react';
```

Change it back to:

```
import React, { Component } from 'react';
```

There should be no more linter errors visible in your editor.

Automating code formatting with Prettier

ESLint can be used to improve any aspect of your code, including how it's formatted. The problem with using something like ESLint for this job is that it only tells you about the formatting issues that it finds. You still have to go fix them.

This is why the ESLint configuration from `create-react-app` doesn't specify any code formatting rules. This is where a tool like Prettier comes in. It's an opinionated code formatter for your JavaScript code. It understands JSX out of the box, so it's ideally suited to format your React components.

The `create-react-app` user guide has a whole section on setting up Git commit hooks that trigger Prettier to format any code before it's committed:
`https://github.com/facebookincubator/create-react-app#user-guide`.

I won't repeat this guide here, but the basic idea is that having Git hooks in place that invoke Prettier on any JavaScript source that's committed will ensure that everything is formatted, well, pretty. The downside to only relying on Git commit hooks is that you as a developer don't necessarily see the formatted code as you're writing it.

In addition to setting up Prettier to format JavaScript source with every commit, adding a code editor plugin can vastly improve the development experience. Once again, you can install the appropriate Atom package (or something similar; Atom is popular so I'm using it as the example editor here):

Once you have the `prettier-atom` package installed, you can use Atom to format your React code. By default, this package uses the key binding *Ctrl + Alt + F* to invoke Prettier to format the current source file. Another option is to enable formatting on save:

Now, every time you save your JavaScript source, Prettier will format it. Let's test it out. First, open up `App.js` and completely trash the formatting so that it looks something like this:

```
                          App.js                  ●
1    import
2    React, { Component } from "react";
3                 import logo from "./logo.svg";
4    import "./App.css";
5
6    class  App extends  Component  {
7      render        () {return (
8         <div className="App">
9        <header className="App-header"     >
10             <img src={logo} className="App-logo" alt="logo" />
11
12             <h1 className="App-title">Welcome to React</h1>
13        </header>
14          <p          className="App-intro">
15            To get started, edit <code>src/App.js</code> and save to reload.
16
17          </p>
18        </div>
19      );
20      }
21    }
22
23    export default App
24    ;
```

Gross! Let's save the file and see what happens:

```
                    App.js

  1  import React, { Component } from 'react';
  2  import logo from './logo.svg';
  3  import './App.css';
  4
  5  class App extends Component {
  6    render() {
  7      return (
  8        <div className="App">
  9          <header className="App-header">
 10            <img src={logo} className="App-logo" alt="logo" />
 11
 12            <h1 className="App-title">Welcome to React</h1>
 13          </header>
 14          <p className="App-intro">
 15            To get started, edit <code>src/App.js</code> and save to reload.
 16          </p>
 17        </div>
 18      );
 19    }
 20  }
 21
 22  export default App;
```

That's way better. Imagine if you had to manually fix that mess. Prettier keeps your code clear with hardly any thought on your part.

Summary

This chapter was all about enforcing the code quality level of your React projects using tools. The first tool you learned about was ESLint. You learned how to install and configure it. Rarely should you have to manually configure ESLint. You learned how to use the ESLint initialization tool that walks you through the various options available for configuring your ESLint rules.

Next, you learned about the different standard ESLint configurations that you can utilize in your React applications. Airbnb is a popular standard you can use with ESLint, and you can customize it rule by rule to fit your team's particular style. You can also tell the ESLint initialization tool that you're planning on using React and have it install the appropriate packages for you.

Finally, you learned how ESLint is used by `create-react-app`. It uses a Webpack plugin to lint your code when the development server is run. You learned how `create-react-app` configures ESLint for this, and how you can use this configuration for your code editor. Prettier is a tool that will automatically format your code so that you don't have to spend time manually addressing lots of ESLint style warnings.

In the next chapter, you'll learn about isolating React component development in their own environments using Storybook.

7
Isolating Components with Storybook

React components are smaller pieces of a larger user interface. Naturally, you want to develop your UI components in tandem with the rest of the application. On the other hand, experimenting with component changes can prove tricky if the only environment you have is inside the larger UI. The focus of this chapter is showing you how the Storybook tool can be leveraged to provide an isolated sandbox for developing React components. You will learn:

- The importance of isolated component development
- Installing Storybook and getting it set up
- Developing components using stories
- Bringing components into the application

The need for isolated component development

Isolating React components during development can be difficult. Often, the only context available to developers and the React components that they're making is the application itself. Rarely do things go exactly as planned while a component is being developed. Part of the debug process for a React component is, well, playing with it.

I often find myself doing weird things in application code to accommodate for temporary changes that we make to components as I troubleshoot problems. For example, I'll change the type of container element to see if this is what's causing the layout issues that I'm seeing; or, I'll change the markup that's internal to the component; or, I'll completely fabricate some state or props that the component uses.

The point is that there are random experiments that you're going to want to perform over the course of developing component. Trying to do this within the application that you're building can be cumbersome. This is mostly because you're forced to take in everything else around the component, which can be distracting when all you care about is seeing what your component does.

Sometimes, I end up creating a whole new page, or a whole new app, just so that I can see what my component does all on its own. This is a painful process and other people feel the same way, which is why **Storybook** exists. React tools exist to automate something for the React developer. With Storybook, you're automating a sandboxed environment for you to work with. It also handles all the build steps for you, so you can just write a story for your components and see the result.

The best way to think about Storybook is as a site like JSFiddle (`https://jsfiddle.net/`) or JSBin (`https://jsbin.com/`). They let you experiment with small pieces of code without having to set up and maintain an environment. Storybook is like JSFiddle for React that exists as an integral part of your project.

Installing and configuring Storybook

The first step to using Storybook is installing the global command-line tool. It's installed as a global tool because it can be used with many projects at the same time, and it can be used to bootstrap new projects. Let's start with this first step:

```
npm install @storybook/cli -g
```

Once this installation is done, you have the command-line tool that's used to modify your `package.json` dependencies and generate boilerplate Storybook files. Let's assume that you've used `create-react-app` to create a new application. Change into your application directory, and use the Storybook command-line tool to add Storybook to your current project:

```
getstorybook
```

The `getstorybook` command does a number of things for you when you run it. Here's what you should see as the output when you run this command:

```
getstorybook - the simplest way to add a storybook to your project.
 • Detecting project type. ✓
 • Adding storybook support to your "Create React App" based project. ✓
 • Preparing to install dependencies. ✓
```

It will try to figure out what type of project you have before adding anything because different types of projects will have different organizational requirements. `getstorybook` takes this into account. Then, it'll install dependencies, boilerplate files, and add scripts to your `package.json`:

```
• Installing dependencies.
To run your storybook, type:
npm run storybook
```

The output tells you have to run the Storybook server within your project. Here's what the `scripts` section of your `package.json` should look like at this point:

```
"scripts": {
  "start": "react-scripts start",
  "build": "react-scripts build",
  "test": "react-scripts test --env=jsdom",
  "eject": "react-scripts eject",
  "storybook": "start-storybook -p 9009 -s public",
  "build-storybook": "build-storybook -s public"
}
```

We'll look at the `build-storybook` script later on in the chapter; you'll use the `storybook` script more often.

Next, let's look at the boilerplate files that `getstorybook` has created for you. First, you'll notice that there's a new `.storybook` directory in the top-level directory of your project:

```
.storybook/
├── addons.js
└── config.js
```

The two files added are as follows:

- `addons.js`: This file imports add-on modules for Storybook. By default, the actions and links add-ons are used, but these can be removed if they're not used.
- `config.js`: This file imports the stories for this project and configures Storybook to use them.

You'll also find a new directory called `stories` within your `src` directory:

```
src/
├──── App.css
├──── App.js
├──── App.test.js
├──── index.css
├──── index.js
├──── logo.svg
├──── registerServiceWorker.js
└──── stories
      └──── index.js
```

Remember how `getstorybook` figured out that you're using `create-react-app` with your project? This is how it knows to put the `stories` directory under `src`. This is where you'll find two demo stories to help get you started:

```
import React from 'react';

import { storiesOf } from '@storybook/react';
import { action } from '@storybook/addon-actions';
import { linkTo } from '@storybook/addon-links';

import { Button, Welcome } from '@storybook/react/demo';

storiesOf('Welcome', module).add('to Storybook', () => (
  <Welcome showApp={linkTo('Button')} />
));

storiesOf('Button', module)
  .add('with text', () => (
    <Button onClick={action('clicked')}>Hello Button</Button>
  ))
  .add('with some emoji', () => (
    <Button onClick={action('clicked')}> 😀 😎 👍 💯 </Button>
  ));
```

Don't worry about figuring out what's going on in this file just yet, we'll get there. These default stories will be replaced by stories that you come up with for your component. It's also helpful to have these default stories in place so that you have something to look at when you fire up the Storybook server for the first time. Let's do that now:

```
npm run storybook
```

After a few seconds, you should see console output that tells you where the server is running so that you can open it in your browser:

```
Storybook started on => http://localhost:9009/
```

Here's what you should see when you look at the Storybook app in your browser:

Here's a rough breakdown of what you're looking at:

- The left pane is where you'll find all of your stories. This is where the two default Storybook stories are displayed.
- The main pane is where you'll see rendered content from the selected story.
- The bottom actions pane is where you'll see triggered actions logged.

Let's try selecting a different story in the left pane:

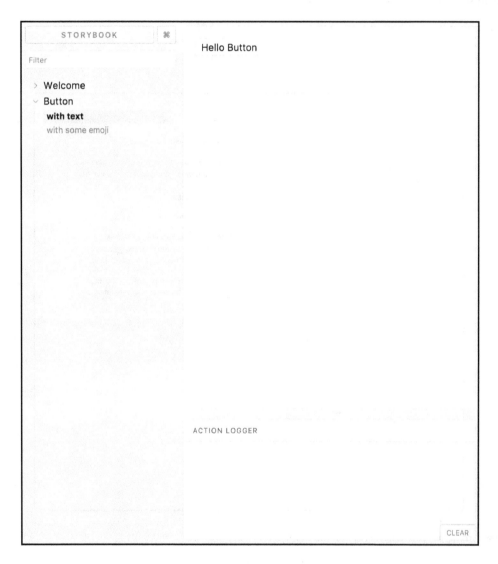

As soon as you change story selections in the left pane, you'll see the rendered component output in the main pane. In this case, it's a basic button.

Developing components with stories

The value of Storybook is that you don't have to set up an application to start hacking components. Or, if you already have an application under development, you don't have to figure out how to integrate in-progress components into your app. Storybook is a tool that enables experimentation. Through the use of add-ons, you can test almost any aspect of your component before worrying about integrating it into your application.

Experimenting with props

Perhaps, the most straightforward way to get started with developing components in Storybook is to start experimenting with different property values. To do so, you just have to create different stories of your component, each with different property values.

First, let's take a look at the component that you're working on:

```
import React from 'react';

const MyComponent = ({ title, content, titleStyle, contentStyle }) => (
  <section>
    <heading>
      <h2 style={titleStyle}>{title}</h2>
    </heading>
    <article style={contentStyle}>{content}</article>
  </section>
);

export default MyComponent;
```

There isn't much to this component. It takes four props and renders some HTML markup. The `title` and the `content` prop values are simple strings. The `titleStyle` and the `contentStyle` props are objects that are assigned to the `style` prop of the appropriate HTML element.

Let's start writing stories for this component. Let's assume that the same approach as the preceding section was used:

1. `create-react-app` is used to create the React application structure and install dependencies
2. `getstorybook` is used to examine the current project and add the appropriate boilerplate and dependencies

You can open up `src/stories/index.js` and get started with the `storiesOf()` function:

```
storiesOf('MyComponent Properties', module)
```

This is the top-level subject that will appear in the left pane when you launch the Storybook UI. Underneath this function is where you add individual stories. Since you're currently interested in testing out different property values, the stories that you add will be for the purpose of reflecting different property values:

```
.add('No Props', () => <MyComponent />)
```

This adds a story called `No Props` to the left pane in Storybook. When you click on it, you'll see what `MyComponent` looks like in the main pane when it's rendered without any props:

There's nothing to see here because both the `title` and the `content` props are missing. Since these two values are the only visible rendered content, there's nothing to display. Let's switch to the next story:

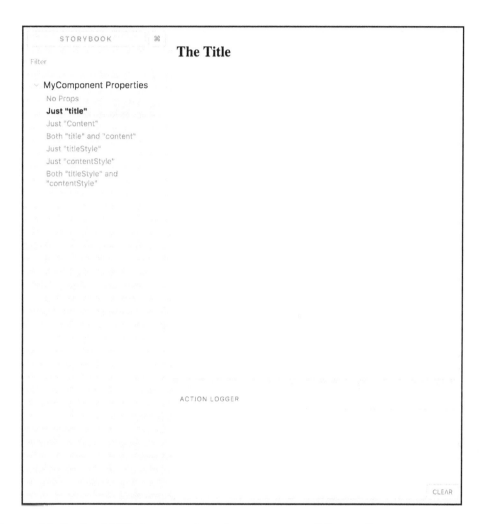

This time, with the **Just "title"** story selected, you can see different React component output rendered. As the story title suggests, only the `title` property is being passed to `MyComponent`. Here's the code for this story:

```
.add('Just "title"', () => <MyComponent title="The Title" />)
```

The next story only passes the `content` property. Here is the result:

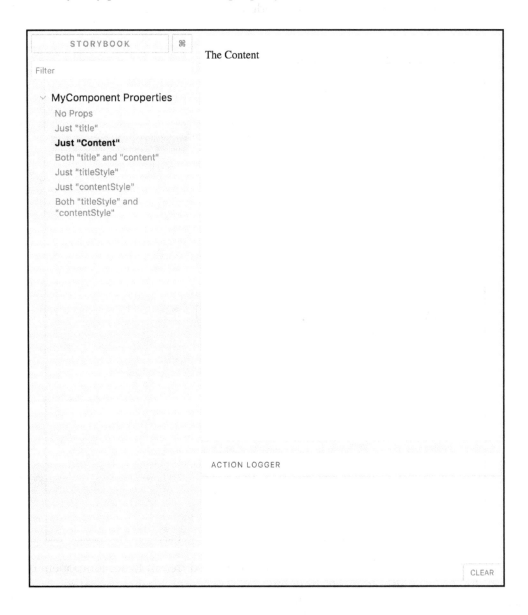

And here is the code that passes just the `content` property:

```
.add('Just "Content"', () => <MyComponent content="The Content" />)
```

The next story passes both the `title` and the `content` properties to `MyComponent`:

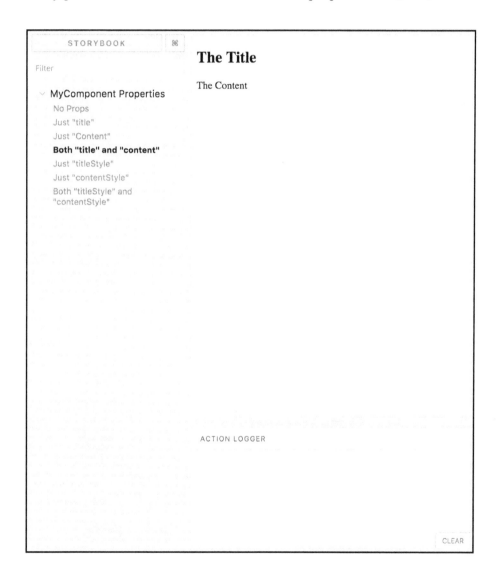

And here is the code that renders both of these props in a story:

```
.add('Both "title" and "content"', () => (
  <MyComponent title="The Title" content="The Content" />
))
```

At this point, you have three stories for your component and they've already proven useful. You've seen how `MyComponent` looks when it's rendered without content or without a title, for example. Based on the result, you might decide to make both of these props mandatory or to provide default values.

Let's move onto the style properties next. First, you'll pass in just the `titleStyle` prop, like so:

```
.add('Just "titleStyle"', () => (
  <MyComponent
    title="The Title"
    content="The Content"
    titleStyle={{ fontWeight: 'normal' }}
  />
))
```

Note that you're also passing the `title` and `content` properties. This way, you can see how the styles actually affect the content that's rendered by `MyComponent`. Here's the result:

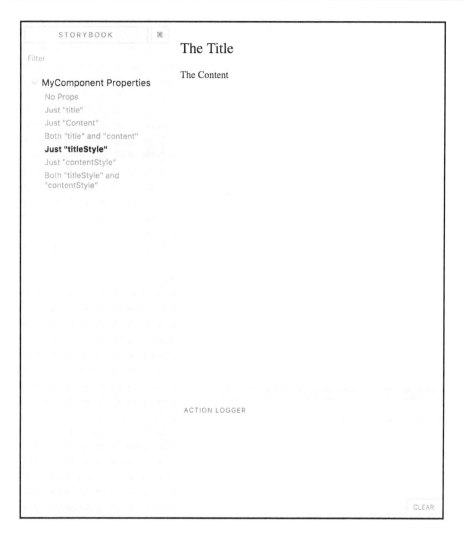

Next, you'll pass just the `contentStyle` prop:

```
.add('Just "contentStyle"', () => (
  <MyComponent
    title="The Title"
    content="The Content"
    contentStyle={{ fontFamily: 'arial', fontSize: '1.2em' }}
  />
))
```

Here's what this looks like:

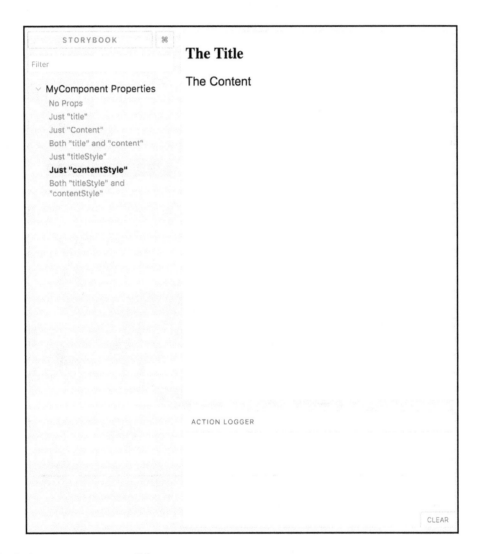

Finally, let's pass every possible prop to `MyComponent`:

```
.add('Both "titleStyle" and "contentStyle"', () => (
  <MyComponent
    title="The Title"
    content="The Content"
```

```
      titleStyle={{ fontWeight: 'normal' }}
      contentStyle={{ fontFamily: 'arial', fontSize: '1.2em' }}
    />
));
```

Here's what `MyComponent` looks like with every prop passed to it:

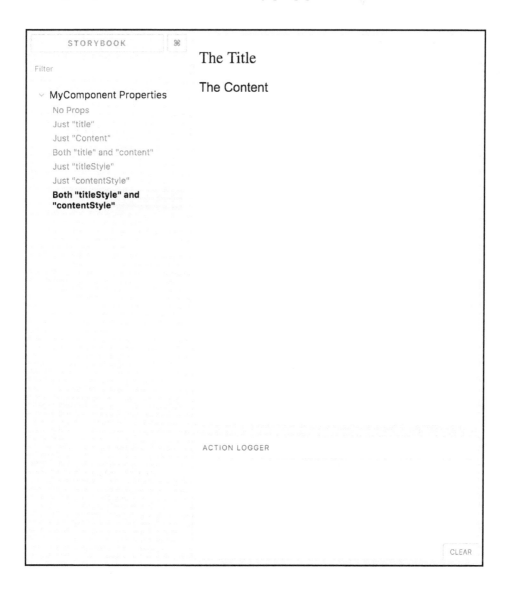

You just created seven stories for a simple component. Using the Storybook dev server and the Storybook user interface, it's easy to toggle between the different stories that you create for your component so that you can easily see the differences between them. This works especially well for functional components that only deal with props, as you just saw.

Here's all of the stories that you just implemented so that you can see what they look like all together:

```
import React from 'react';
import { storiesOf } from '@storybook/react';
import MyComponent from '../MyComponent';

storiesOf('MyComponent Properties', module)
  .add('No Props', () => <MyComponent />)
  .add('Just "title"', () => <MyComponent title="The Title" />)
  .add('Just "Content"', () => <MyComponent content="The Content" />)
  .add('Both "title" and "content"', () => (
    <MyComponent title="The Title" content="The Content" />
  ))
  .add('Just "titleStyle"', () => (
    <MyComponent
      title="The Title"
      content="The Content"
      titleStyle={{ fontWeight: 'normal' }}
    />
  ))
  .add('Just "contentStyle"', () => (
    <MyComponent
      title="The Title"
      content="The Content"
      contentStyle={{ fontFamily: 'arial', fontSize: '1.2em' }}
    />
  ))
  .add('Both "titleStyle" and "contentStyle"', () => (
    <MyComponent
      title="The Title"
      content="The Content"
      titleStyle={{ fontWeight: 'normal' }}
      contentStyle={{ fontFamily: 'arial', fontSize: '1.2em' }}
    />
  ));
```

What's nice about adding stories where each one has a different prop configuration for your component is that it's like taking a static snapshot of your component. Then, once you have several stories for your component, you can toggle between the snapshots. On the other hand, you might not be ready to start implementing several stories this way just yet. If you just want to fiddle around with prop values, there's a Storybook add-on called **Knobs**.

The Knobs add-on allows you to play with React component prop values through form controls in the Storybook UI. Let's try out this add-on now. The first step is installing it in your project:

```
npm install @storybook/addon-knobs --save-dev
```

Then, you have to tell your Storybook configuration that you want to use the add-on. Add the following line to .storybook/addons.js:

```
import '@storybook/addon-knobs/register';
```

Now you can import the withKnobs decorator into your stories/index.js file, which is used to tell Storybook that the stories that follow will use controls to play with prop values. You'll also want to import the various types of knob controls. These are simple functions that pass values to your components as the values in the Storybook UI change.

As an example, let's copy the same storyline as you just implemented for MyComponent. This time, instead of building a whole bunch of static stories where each one sets particular property values, you'll just add one story that uses the Knobs add-on to control prop values. Here is what you'll need to add as imports:

```
import { withKnobs, text, object } from '@storybook/addon-knobs/react';
```

Here is the new context for stories, along with a default story that uses knob controls to set and change your React component property values:

```
storiesOf('MyComponent Prop Knobs', module)
  .addDecorator(withKnobs)
  .add('default', () => (
    <MyComponent
      title={text('Title', 'The Title')}
      content={text('Content', 'The Content')}
      titleStyle={object('Title Style', { fontWeight: 'normal' })}
      contentStyle={object('Content Style', {
        fontFamily: 'arial',
        fontSize: '1.2em'
      })}
    />
  ));
```

The two functions that you imported from the Knobs add-on, `text()` and `object()`, are used to set the label for a knob control, and a default value. For example, `title` is using the `text()` function with a default string value, while `contentStyle` is using the `object()` function with a default style object.

Here's what the result looks like in the Storybook user interface:

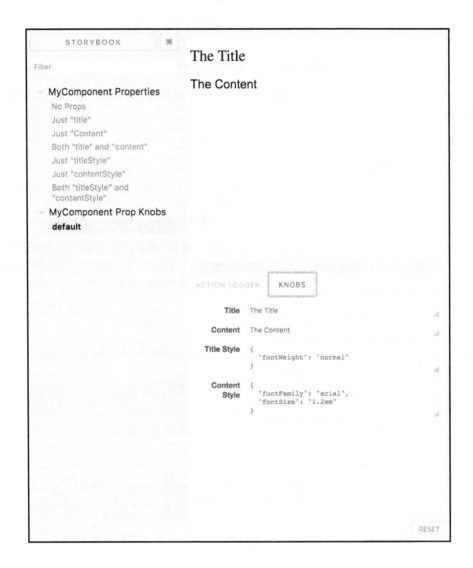

If you look at the bottom pane, you'll see that there's a **KNOBS** tab beside the **ACTION LOGGER** tab. Based on the functions from the Knobs add-on that you used to declare your story, these form controls are created. Now you can go ahead and play around with component prop values and watch the rendered content change on the fly:

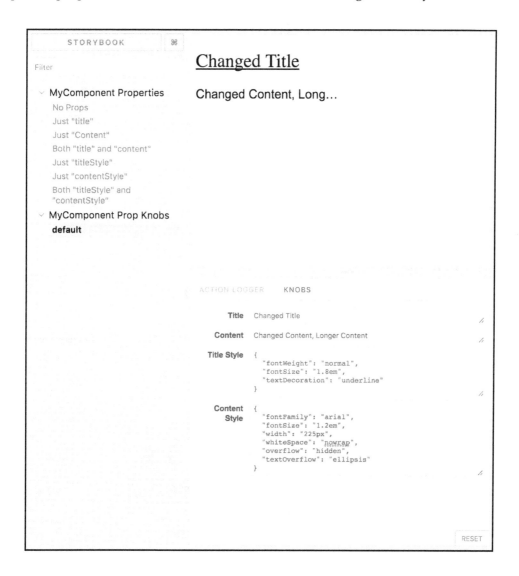

If you end up finding prop values that you like, while experimenting with knob fields, you take these values and hardcode them into a story. It's like bookmarking a component configuration that works so that you can go back to it later on.

Experimenting with actions

Let's shift our attention to another add-on—Actions. This add-on is enabled in your Storybook by default. The idea with Actions is that once you select a story, you can interact with the rendered page elements in the main pane. Actions provide you with a mechanism that logs user interactions in the Storybook UI. Additionally, Actions can serve as a general-purpose tool to help you monitor data as it flows through your components.

Let's start with a simple button component:

```
import React from 'react';

const MyButton = ({ onClick }) => (
  <button onClick={onClick}>My Button</button>
);

export default MyButton;
```

The `MyButton` component re

nders a `<button>` element and assigns it an `onClick` event handler. The handler is actually defined by `MyComponent`; it's passed in as a prop. So let's create a story for this component and pass it an `onClick` handler function:

```
import React from 'react';
import { storiesOf } from '@storybook/react';
import { action } from '@storybook/addon-actions';
import MyButton from '../MyButton';

storiesOf('MyButton', module).add('clicks', () => (
  <MyButton onClick={action('my component clicked')} />
));
```

Do you see the `action()` function that's imported from `@storybook/addon-actions`? This is a higher-order function—a function that returns another function. When you call `action('my component clicked')`, you're getting a new function in return. The new function behaves kind of like `console.log()`, in that you can assign it a label and log arbitrary values. The difference is that functions created by the Storybook `action()` add-on function is that the output is rendered right in the actions pane of the Storybook UI:

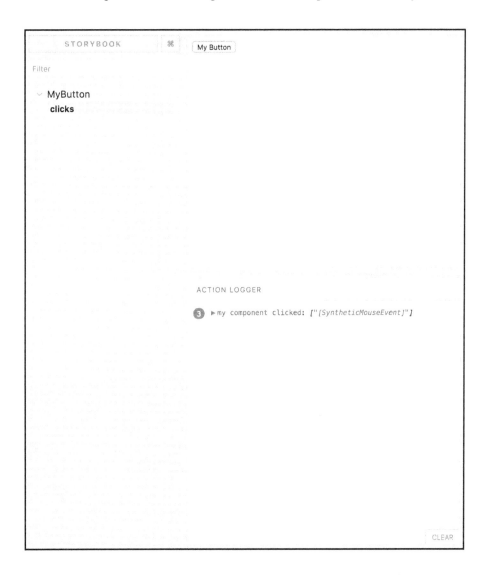

As usual, the <button> element is rendered in the main pane. The content that you're seeing in the actions pane is the result of clicking on the button three times. The output is the exact same with every click, so the output is all grouped under the my component clicked label that you assigned to the handler function.

In the preceding example, the event handler functions that action() creates are useful for as a substitute for actual event handler functions that you would pass to your components. Other times, you actually need the event handling behavior to run. For example, you have a controlled form field that maintains its own state and you want to see what happens as the state changes.

For cases like these, I find the simplest and most effective approach is to add event handler props, even if you're not using them for anything else. Let's take a look at an example of this:

```jsx
import React, { Component } from 'react';

class MyRangeInput extends Component {
  static defaultProps = {
    onChange() {},
    onRender() {}
  };

  state = { value: 25 };

  onChange = ({ target: { value } }) => {
    this.setState({ value });
    this.props.onChange(value);
  };

  render() {
    const { value } = this.state;
    this.props.onRender(value);
    return (
      <input
        type="range"
        min="1"
        max="100"
        value={value}
        onChange={this.onChange}
      />
    );
  }
}
export default MyRangeInput;
```

Let's start by taking a look at the `defaultProps` of this component. By default, this component has two default handler functions for `onChange` and `onRender`—these do nothing so that if they're not set, they can still be called and nothing will happen. As you might have guessed, we can now pass `action()` handlers to `MyRangeInput` components. Let's try this out. Here's what your `stories/index.js` looks like now:

```
import React from 'react';
import { storiesOf } from '@storybook/react';
import { action } from '@storybook/addon-actions';
import MyButton from '../MyButton';
import MyRangeInput from '../MyRangeInput';

storiesOf('MyButton', module).add('clicks', () => (
  <MyButton onClick={action('my component clicked')} />
));

storiesOf('MyRangeInput', module).add('slides', () => (
  <MyRangeInput
    onChange={action('range input changed')}
    onRender={action('range input rendered')}
  />
));
```

Now when you view this story in the Storybook UI, you should see lots of actions logged when you slide the range input slider:

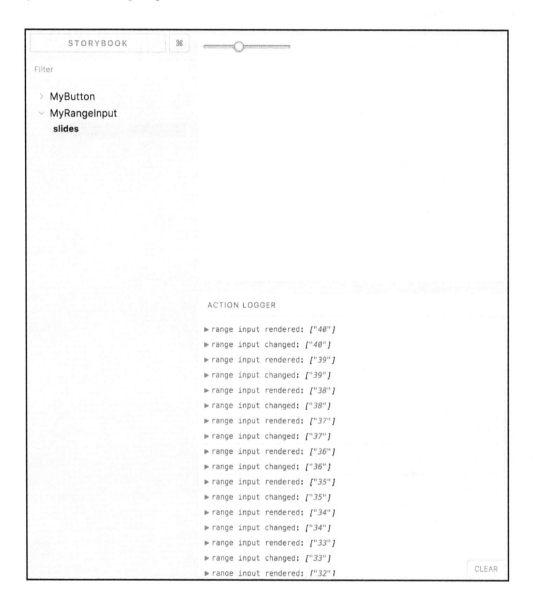

As the slider handle moves, you can see the two event handler functions that you've passed to the component are logging the value at different stages of the component rendering life cycle. The most recent action is logged at the top of the pane, unlike browser dev tools which logs the most recent value at the bottom.

Let's revisit the `MyRangeInput` code for a moment. The first function that's called when the slider handle moves is the change handler:

```
onChange = ({ target: { value } }) => {
  this.setState({ value });
  this.props.onChange(value);
};
```

This `onChange()` method is internal to `MyRangeInput`. It's needed because the `<input>` element that it renders uses the component state as the single source of truth. These are called controlled components in React terminology. First, it sets the state of the value using the `target.value` property from the event argument. Then, it calls `this.props.onChange()`, passing it the same value. This is how you can see the even value in the Storybook UI.

Note that this isn't the right place to log the updated state of the component. When you call `setState()`, you have to make the assumption that you're done dealing with state in the function because it doesn't always update synchronously. Calling `setState()` only schedules the state update and the subsequent re-render of your component.

Here's an example of how this can cause problems. Let's say that instead of logging the value from the event argument, you logged the value state after setting it:

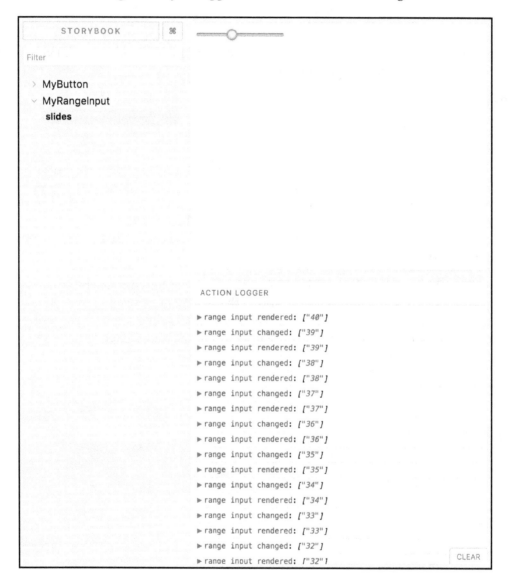

There's a bit of a problem here now. The `onChange` handler is logging the old state while the `onRender` handler is logging the updated state. This sort of logging output is super confusing if you're trying to trace an event value to rendered output—things don't line up! Never log state values after calling `setState()`.

If the idea of calling noop functions makes you feel uncomfortable, then maybe this approach to displaying actions in Storybook isn't for you. On the other hand, you might find that having a utility to log essentially anything at any point in the life cycle of your component without the need to write a bunch of debugging code inside your component. For such cases, Actions are the way to go.

Linking stories together

The Links Storybook add-on allows you to link stories together in the same way that you would link regular web pages together. Storybook has a navigation pane that allows you to switch from story to story. This is useful as a table of contents. But when you're reading content on the web, you typically find several links in a single paragraph of text. Imagine if the only way to move around on the web were to look through the links in the table of contents in each document, it'd be painful.

For the same reason that embedding links within content on the web is valuable, embedding links in Storybook output is valuable: they provide context. Let's take a look at an example of links in action. Like Actions, the links add-on is enabled by default when you run the `getstorybook` command in your project. Here's the component that you'll write stories for:

```
import React from 'react';

const MyComponent = ({ headingText, children }) => (
  <section>
    <header>
      <h1>{headingText}</h1>
    </header>
    <article>{children}</article>
  </section>
);

MyComponent.defaultProps = {
  headingText: 'Heading Text'
};

export default MyComponent;
```

This component accepts `headingText` and `children` properties. Now let's write some Storybook stories that are linked together. Here are three stories that are all linked to each other within the output pane:

```jsx
import React from 'react';
import { storiesOf } from '@storybook/react';
import { linkTo } from '@storybook/addon-links';
import LinkTo from '@storybook/addon-links/react';
import MyComponent from '../MyComponent';

storiesOf('MyComponent', module)
  .add('default', () => (
    <section>
      <MyComponent />
      <p>
        This is the default. You can also change the{' '}
        <LinkTo story="heading text">heading text</LinkTo>.
      </p>
    </section>
  ))
  .add('heading text', () => (
    <section>
      <MyComponent headingText="Changed Heading!" />
      <p>
        This time, a custom <code>headingText</code> prop
        changes the heading text. You can also pass{' '}
        <LinkTo story="children">child elements</LinkTo> to{' '}
        <code>MyComponent</code>.
      </p>
      <button onClick={linkTo('default')}>Default</button>
    </section>
  ))
  .add('children', () => (
    <section>
      <MyComponent>
        <strong>Child Element</strong>
      </MyComponent>
      <p>
        Passing a child component. You can also change the{' '}
        <LinkTo story="headingText">heading text</LinkTo> of{' '}
        <code>MyComponent</code>.
      </p>
      <button onClick={linkTo('default')}>Default</button>
    </section>
  ));
```

Let's walk through each of these stories so that you can see how they're linked to each other. First, there's the default story:

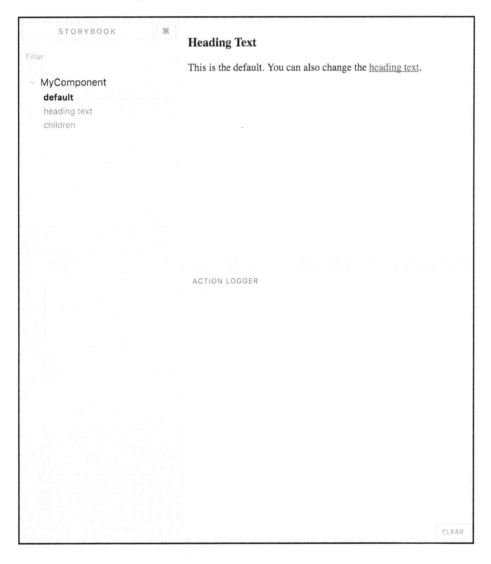

You can see the rendered content of `MyComponent`, which consists only of heading text because you didn't pass it any children. Moreover, this is just the default heading text, as the content rendered below the component explains. The content handily links to a story that renders different heading text:

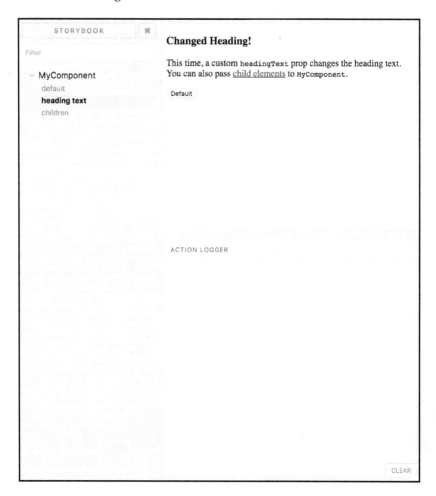

Once again, you can see the rendered component with the custom `headingText` prop value and a note below the component that links to another story. In this case, the link takes the user to a story that passes a child element to `MyComponent`:

```
<LinkTo story="children">child elements</LinkTo>
```

There's also a button that uses the `linkTo()` function to build a callback function that takes the user to the linked story instead of the `<LinkTo>` component which renders a link:

```
<button onClick={linkTo('default')}>Default</button>
```

Both approaches take a kind argument, but they're omitted here because we're linking from within the `MyComponent` kind. The ability to link stories together like this takes you a step closer to using Storybook as a tool for documenting your React components.

Stories as documentation

Storybook is much more than a convenient place to isolate your components while they're developed. With add-ons, it's also an effective tool for documenting your components. As your application grows, it's all the more compelling to have something like Storybook in place. Other developers are likely going to have to work with components that you've created. Wouldn't it be nice if they could look at Storybook stories to see the various ways your component can be used?

The last add-on that we'll look at in this chapter is called Info. It provides usage info about the component in a nicely-presented format, in addition to the standard rendered component output.

Let's create a couple of components that we want to document. Instead of writing every story in `stories/index.js` like you have been throughout this chapter, let's separate your stories into something more consumable:

- `stories/MyButton.story.js`
- `stories/MyList.story.js`

The stories for the two components that you're about to implement will be separated in their own modules, which will be a little easier to maintain going forward. Another change that you'll have to make in order to support this new file layout is in `.storybook/config.js`. Here, you'll have to require your two story modules individually:

```
import { configure } from '@storybook/react';

function loadStories() {
  require('../src/stories/MyButton.story');
  require('../src/stories/MyList.story');
}
configure(loadStories, module);
```

Let's take a look at the components now. First, there's `MyButton`:

```
import React from 'react';
import PropTypes from 'prop-types';

const MyButton = ({ onClick }) => (
  <button onClick={onClick}>My Button</button>
);

MyButton.propATypes = {
  onClick: PropTypes.func
};

export default MyButton;
```

You can see that `MyButton` defines a `propTypes` property; you'll see why this is important for the Info Storybook add-on shortly. Next, let's look at the `MyList` component:

```
import React from 'react';
import PropTypes from 'prop-types';

const Empty = ({ items, children }) =>
  items.length === 0 ? children : null;

const MyList = ({ items }) => (
  <section>
    <Empty items={items}>No items found</Empty>
    <ul>{items.map((v, i) => <li key={i}>{v}</li>)}</ul>
  </section>
);

MyList.propTypes = {
  items: PropTypes.array
};

MyList.defaultProps = {
  items: []
};
export default MyList;
```

This component also defines a `propTypes` property. It defines a `defaultProps` property as well so that when the `items` property isn't provided, it has an empty array by default so that the call to `map()` still works.

Now you're ready to write stories for these two components. Keeping in mind that you also want these stories to serve as the main source of documentation for your components, you'll use the Info add-on for Storybook to give users more usage information for any given story. Let's start with MyButton.story.js:

```
import React from 'react';
import { storiesOf } from '@storybook/react';
import { withInfo } from '@storybook/addon-info';
import { action } from '@storybook/addon-actions';
import MyButton from '../MyButton';

storiesOf('MyButton', module)
  .add(
    'basic usage',
    withInfo('
      Without passing any properties
    ')(() => <MyButton />)
  )
  .add(
    'click handler',
    withInfo('
      Passing an event handler function that's called when
      the button is clicked
    ')(() => <MyButton onClick={action('button clicked')} />)
  );
```

Here, you're documenting MyButton using two stories, each of which show a different way to use the component. The first story shows the basic usage and the second story shows how to pass a click handler property. The new addition to these stories is the call to withInfo(). This function is from the Info Storybook add-on, and you can pass it some text (markdown supported) that goes into more detail about the story. In other words, this is where you document a specific use of your component.

Now let's look at MyList.story.js before we see what the output of the Info add-on looks like in the Storybook UI:

```
import React from 'react';
import { storiesOf } from '@storybook/react';
import { withInfo } from '@storybook/addon-info';
import MyList from '../MyList';

storiesOf('MyList', module)
  .add(
    'basic usage',
    withInfo('
      Without passing any properties
```

```
    ')(() => <MyList />)
  )
  .add(
    'passing an array of items',
    withInfo('
      Passing an array to the items property
    ')(() => <MyList items={['first', 'second', 'third']} />)
  );
```

This looks a lot like the stories defined for `MyButton`—different docs and components, same overall structure and approach.

Let's take a look at the default usage story for `MyButton`:

As expected, the button is rendered in the output pane so that users can see what they're working with. In the top-right corner of the output pane, there's an info button. When you click on it, you see all of the extra info provided by calling `withInfo()` in your story:

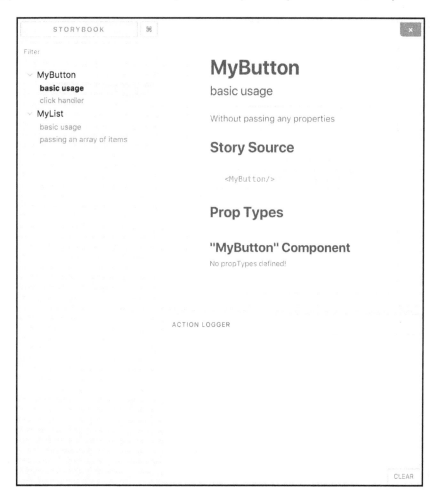

This reveals all sorts of information about the story, and the component that you're documenting. From top to bottom, here is what it displays:

- Component name
- Story name
- Usage documentation (provided as an argument to `withInfo()`)

- Source used to render component
- Properties available to component (read from `propTypes`)

The nice thing about the Info add-on is that it shows your users the source used to render the output that they're looking at, and shows the available properties if you provide them as prop types. This means that someone who is trying to understand and use your components can get the information they need without you, the component author, putting in a ton of extra effort.

Let's take a look at the `MyList` component when it's passed an array of items:

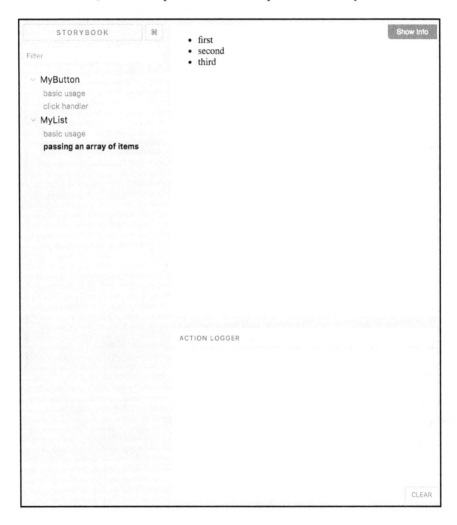

It renders a list of items that it gets through a prop. Let's look at the info for this story now:

By looking at the information about this story, you can see at a glance the props that this component accepts, what their default values are, and the code that was used to generate the example, all in one place. I also like the fact that the info pane is hidden by default, meaning that you can navigate through stories and look for the end result that you need, and only then worry about the details.

Building static Storybook apps

If you're building component library that you either want to distribute as an open source project or as something that's shared with various teams within your organization, you can use Storybook as the tool that documents how to work with your components. That said, you might not want to have a Storybook server running or you might just want to host the Storybook documentation.

In either scenario, you need a static build of the stories that you've written for your component library. Storybook provides you with this utility when you run the `getstorybook` command.

Let's continue with the example from the preceding section where you used Storybook to document the usage scenarios of your two components. To build your static Storybook documentation, all you have to do is run the following command from within your project directory:

```
npm run build-storybook
```

You should see output that looks like the following:

```
info @storybook/react v3.3.13
info
info => Loading custom addons config.
info => Using default webpack setup based on "Create React App".
info => Copying static files from: public
info Building storybook ...
```

Once built, you'll see a new `storybook-static` directory in your project folder. Inside, you'll see several files, including the static JavaScript bundles created by Webpack and an `index.html` file that you can serve from any web server or simply open directly in your web browser.

Summary

This chapter was the focus of a tool called Storybook. Storybook provides React developers with a sandboxed environment that makes it easy to develop React components on their own. This can be difficult when the only environment you have is the application that you're working on. Storybook provides a level of development isolation.

First, you learned how to install the global Storybook command-line utility and how to use this utility to get Storybook set up in your `create-react-app` projects. Next, you learned how to write stories that show different perspectives of a component.

Then, you learned that a good portion of Storybook functionality comes from add-ons. You learned that Actions help with logging and that links provide a mechanism for navigation beyond the default. You also learned how to write documentation for React components using Storybook. We closed the chapter with a look at building static Storybook content.

In the next chapter, you'll explore the React tooling available within web browsers.

Debugging Components in the Browser

8

If you're developing a React web application, you need browser-based tooling to help you see what's happening on the page from the perspective of a React developer. Web browsers today have amazing developer tools installed by default. These are essential if you're doing any kind of web development because they expose what's really going on in terms of DOM, styles, performance, network requests, you name it.

With React, you still need all of this tooling, but you need more than that. The core tenet of React is declarative markup within JavaScript components. If this abstraction isn't present in the web browser tooling that developers rely on for everything else, life is more difficult than it needs to be.

In this chapter, you'll learn:

- Installing the React Developer Tools browser add-on
- Locating and selecting React components
- Manipulating component props and state
- Profiling component performance

Installing the React Developer Tools add-on

The first step to getting started with React tooling is to install the React Developer Tools browser extension. I'll be using Chrome in the examples throughout this chapter as this is a popular choice. React Developer Tools is also available as an extension for Firefox (`https://addons.mozilla.org/en-US/firefox/addon/react-devtools/`).

To get the extension installed in Chrome, visit `https://chrome.google.com/webstore/category/extensions` and search for `react developer tools`:

The first result should be the extension that you want. Click on the **ADD TO CHROME** button to install it:

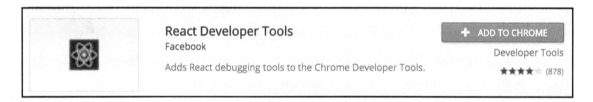

Chrome might warn you that it can change data on websites that you visit. Don't worry, the extension is only activated when you visit React apps:

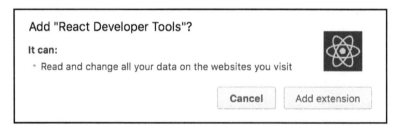

Once you click on the **Add extension** button, the extension is marked as installed:

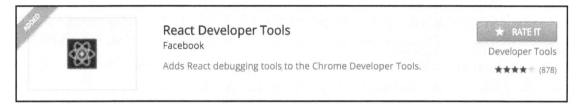

You're all set! With the React Developer Tools Chrome extension installed and enabled, you're ready to start inspecting React components on the page, just like you would with regular DOM elements.

Working with React elements in React Developer Tools

Once you've installed React Developer Tools in Chrome, you'll see a button in the toolbar located to the right of the browser address bar. Here's what mine looks like:

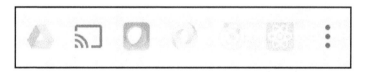

I have several buttons for browser extensions here. You can see the React Developer Tools button at the far right—the one with the React logo. When the button is greyed-out like this, it means that you're not currently on a page running a React application. Go ahead and try clicking on it while you're on some random page:

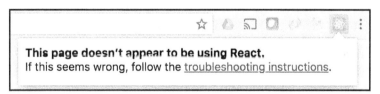

Now let's use `create-react-app` to create a new application, the same process you've been following throughout this book:

```
create-react-app finding-and-selecting-components
```

Now fire up the development server:

```
npm start
```

This should take you directly to the browser page with your React application loaded up in a new tab. Now the React Developer Tools button should look different:

There you go. Since you're on a page that's running a React application, the React Developer Tools button comes alive to let you know that it's available. Try clicking on it now:

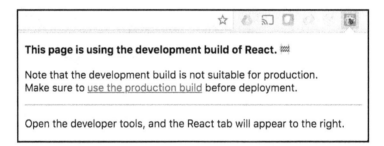

Awesome! The React Developer Tools can detect that this is a development build of the React library. This could come in handy in case you ever find yourself in a situation where you accidentally deploy the development build of React to a production environment. Admittedly, this is more difficult to do today with tools like `create-react-app` where you have the tooling in place to build production versions for free.

Okay, so now that you have your React browser tooling in place, what else can it do for you other than detect the type of React build that's being used by a given app? Let's open up the developer tools pane within Chrome and find out:

You can see all of the regular sections that you normally see in the developer tools pane: **Elements**, **Console**, and so on. But there's nothing about React? I happen to have my developer tools pane docked to the right-hand side of my browser window, so you can't see every section. If you're seeing the same thing, you just have to click on the arrow button next to **Performance**:

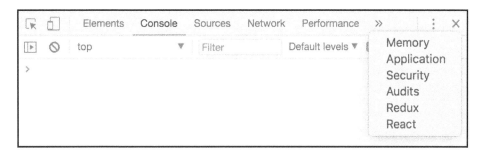

Select **React** from the menu and you'll be taken to the React section of the developer tools panel. Once it loads, you should see the root React component displayed:

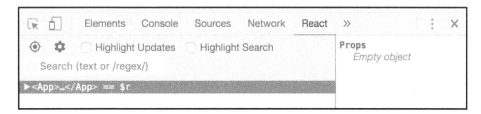

If you've used the DOM inspector tool in any browser, this interface should feel familiar. In the main section to the left, you have your React element tree. This should closely resemble your JSX source. To the right of this tree, you have details of the currently-selected element, in this case it's App, and it doesn't define any properties.

If you expand `App`, you'll see its child HTML markup and other React elements:

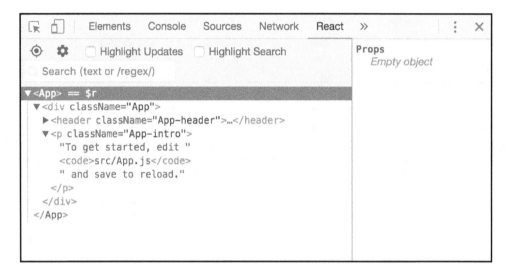

This is the default source code after running `create-react-app`, so there isn't very much of interest under the `App` element. To further explore React Developer Tools, you'll have to introduce some more components and render more React elements on the page.

Selecting React elements

There are actually two ways to select a React element using React Developer tools. When you open the React section of the developer tools pane, the root element of the React app is automatically selected in the element tree. However, you can expand this element to reveal child elements and select them.

Let's put together a simple app that will help you explore the rendered React elements on the page using React Developer Tools. Starting from the top level, here's the `App` component:

```
import React from 'react';
import MyContainer from './MyContainer';
import MyChild from './MyChild';

const App = () => (
  <MyContainer>
```

```
      <MyChild>child text</MyChild>
    </MyContainer>
  );

  export default App;
```

By looking at this source, you can take a glimpse at the overall structure of the React elements when they're rendered on the page. Next, let's look at the `MyContainer` component:

```
import React from 'react';
import './MyContainer.css';

const MyContainer = ({ children }) => (
  <section className="MyContainer">
    <header>
      <h1>Container</h1>
    </header>
    <article>{children}</article>
  </section>
);

export default MyContainer;
```

This component renders some header text and whatever children are passed to it. In this application, you're passing it a `MyChild` element, so let's look at this component next:

```
import React from 'react';

const MyChild = ({ children }) => <p>{children}</p>;

export default MyChild;
```

Now when you run `npm start`, you should see the following content rendered:

Not much to look at, but you know that everything is working as expected. The app is small enough that you can see every JSX element within the tree view of the React Developer Tools pane:

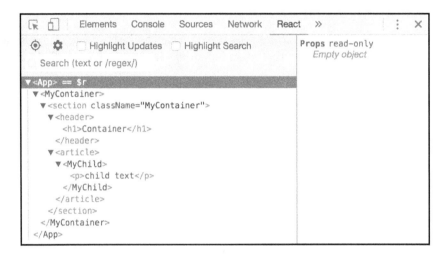

There is a visual distinction between React elements and other element types, so that they're easier to spot in this tree view. For example, the <MyContainer> element is in one color while the <section> element is in a different color. Let's select the <MyContainer> element and see what happens:

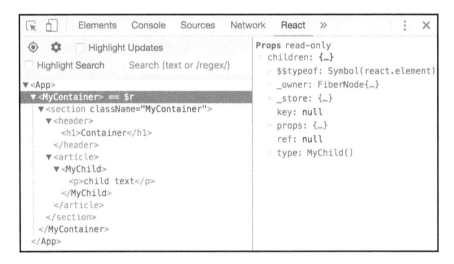

Up until this point, you've only had the <App> element selected, so there wasn't anything to show about this element—it has no props or state. The <MyContainer> element, on the other hand, does have properties to show. In this case, it has a children property because a <MyChild> element was rendered as a child element of <MyContainer>. Don't worry about the specifics displayed to the right of the selected element just yet—we'll go into more detail in the next section.

Next, let's activate the selection tool. It's the button above element tree that has a target icon in it. When you click on the icon, it changes to blue to let you know that it's active:

The idea of this tool is to allow you to click elements on the page and have the corresponding React component selected in the developer tools pane. You'll notice that when the tool is active, elements are highlighted as you move over them, letting you know what they are:

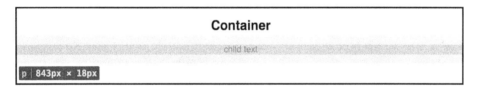

Here, the mouse pointer is over the <p> element on the page, as the little box indicates. If you click on the element, the selection tool will select the appropriate element in the developer tools pane and then deactivate itself. Here's what the <p> element looks like when selected:

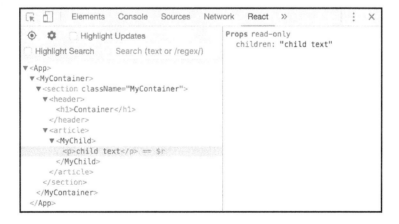

Even though the <p> element is selected here, you're seeing props from the React element that rendered it—<MyChild>. If you're working with page elements and you're not exactly sure which React element rendered them, using the selection tool in React Developer Tools is a quick way to find out.

Searching for React elements

When your application gets bigger, traversing elements on the page or in the element tree in the React Developer Tools panel doesn't work so well. You need a way to search for React elements. Luckily, there's a search box located right above the element tree:

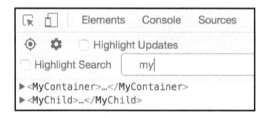

As you type in the search box, elements are filtered in the element tree below. As you can see, the matching text is also highlighted. The search only matches against the name of the element, which means that searching will not help you if you need to filter down from 100 of the same type of element. However, even in these cases, searching can remove everything else in the app, so that you have a smaller list to manually go through.

If you select the **Highlight Search** checkbox, searching will highlight React elements in the main browser window:

Both React elements (<MyContainer> and <MyChild>) on this page are highlighted because they both match the search criteria, my. Let's see what happens when you search for child instead:

This time, you can see the only React element that matches your search. It's highlighted in the main browser window and in the element tree. By searching like this, you know exactly what element on the screen you're working with when you select it in the element tree.

Inspecting component properties and state

React follows a declarative paradigm so it helps to have tooling in place like React Developer Tools that lets you see your JSX markup in the browser. This is only the static aspect of your React app—you declare the elements of your UI and let data control the rest. Using the same tool, you can watch props and state as they flow through your app. To demonstrate this, let's create a simple list that fills itself up once mounted:

```
import React, { Component } from 'react';
import MyItem from './MyItem';

class MyList extends Component {
  timer = null;
  state = { items: [] };
  componentDidMount() {
    this.timer = setInterval(() => {
      if (this.state.items.length === 10) {
        clearInterval(this.timer);
        return;
      }

      this.setState(state => ({
        ...state,
        items: [
          ...state.items,
          {
            label: 'Item ${state.items.length + 1}',
            strikethrough: false
          }
        ]
      }));
    }, 3000);
  }

  componentWillUnmount() {
    clearInterval(this.timer);
  }

  onItemClick = index => () => {
    this.setState(state => ({
```

```
        ...state,
        items: state.items.map(
          (v, i) =>
            index === i
              ? {
                  ...v,
                  strikethrough: !v.strikethrough
                }
              : v
        )
      }));
    };

    render() {
      return (
        <ul>
          {this.state.items.map((v, i) => (
            <MyItem
              key={i}
              label={v.label}
              strikethrough={v.strikethrough}
              onClick={this.onItemClick(i)}

            />
          ))}
        </ul>
      );
    }
  }

  export default MyList;
```

Here's a rough breakdown of everything that this component does:

- `timer` and `state`: These properties are initialized. The main state of this component is an `items` array.
- `componentDidMount()`: Sets up an interval timer that adds a new value to the `items` array every three seconds. Once there are ten items, the interval is cleared.
- `componentWillUnmount()`: Makes sure the `timer` property is forcefully cleared.

- onItemClick(): Takes an index argument and returns an event handler for the index. When the handler is called, the strikethrough state is toggled.
- render(): Renders a <ul> list of <MyItem> elements, passing it relevant props.

The idea here is to slowly build the list so that you can watch the state changes happen in the browser tooling. Then, with the MyList elements, you can watch the props that are passed to it. Here's what this component looks like:

```
import React from 'react';

const MyItem = ({ label, strikethrough, onClick }) => (
  <li
    style={{
      cursor: 'pointer',
      textDecoration: strikethrough ? 'line-through' : 'none'
    }}
    onClick={onClick}
  >
    {label}
  </li>
);

export default MyItem;
```

It's a simple list item. The textDecoration style changes based on the value of the strikethrough prop. When this is true, the text will appear to be striked out.

Let's load up this app in your browser and watch the state of MyList change as the interval handler is called. Once the app loads, make sure you have the React Developer Tools pane open and ready to go. Then, expand the <App> element and select <MyList>. You'll see the state of the element to the right:

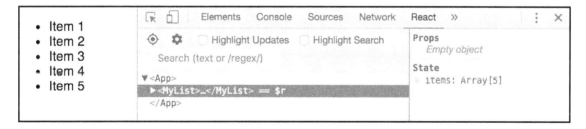

The rendered content to the left matches the state displayed to the right for the selected `<MyList>` element. There's an array of 5 items, and a list of 5 items is rendered on the page. This example uses an interval timer to update the state over time (until it reaches 10 items). If you watch closely, you can see that the state value to the right changes in sync with the rendered content, as new list items are added. You can also expand individual items in the state to see their values:

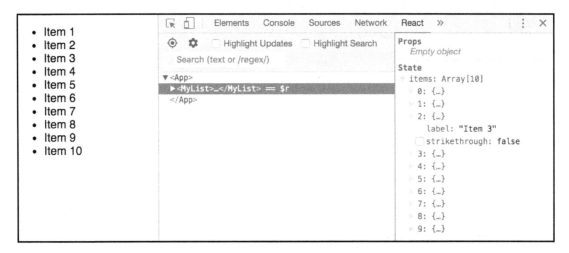

If you expand the `<MyList>` element, you'll see all of the `<MyItem>` elements rendered as a result of items being added to the `items` array state. From there, you can select `<MyItem>` elements to view its props and state. In this example, the `<MyItem>` elements only have props—no state:

You can see the props passed to a given element in the tree view to the left. This is a little difficult to read though, compared to the values you can see to the right that show you the prop values of the selected element. The following props are passed to <MyItem>:

- label: The text to be rendered
- onClick: The function that's called when the item is clicked
- strikethrough: If true, the text is rendered with a strikethrough style

You can watch the values of properties change as elements are re-rendered. In the case of this app, when you click on a list item, the handler function will change the state of the items list in the <MyList> element. Specifically, the index of the item clicked will toggle its strikethrough value. This in turn will cause the <MyItem> element to re-render itself with the new prop value. If you keep the element that you're about to click on selected in the developer tools pane, you can keep an eye on props as they change:

The text for the first item is rendered with the strikethrough style. This is because the strikethrough property is true. If you look closely at the prop values to the right of the element tree in the developer tools pane, you can see individual props flash yellow when they change—a visual cue that's handy for debugging your components.

Manipulating element state values

React Developer Tools lets you inspect the current state of elements that you select. You can also monitor state changes as they happen, as was demonstrated in the preceding section where you had set up an interval timer that changed the state of your element over time. The state of an element can also be manipulated in limited ways.

For this next example, let's modify the `MyList` component to remove the interval timer and simply populate the state when it's constructed:

```
import React, { Component } from 'react';
import MyItem from './MyItem';
class MyList extends Component {
  timer = null;
  state = {
    items: new Array(10).fill(null).map((v, i) => ({
      label: 'Item ${i + 1}',
      strikethrough: false
    }))
  };

  onItemClick = index => () => {
    this.setState(state => ({
      ...state,
      items: state.items.map(
        (v, i) =>
          index === i
            ? {
                ...v,
                strikethrough: !v.strikethrough
              }
            : v
      )
    }));
  };

  render() {
    return (
      <ul>
        {this.state.items.map((v, i) => (
          <MyItem
            key={i}
            label={v.label}
            strikethrough={v.strikethrough}
            onClick={this.onItemClick(i)}
          />
```

```
      ) ) }
    </ul>
  );
  }
}

export default MyList;
```

Now when you run this app, you'll see the 10 items rendered immediately. Other than this, there are no other changes. You can still click on individual items to toggle their `strikethrough` state. Once you have this app up and running, make sure the React Developer Tools browser pane is open so that you can select the `<MyList>` element:

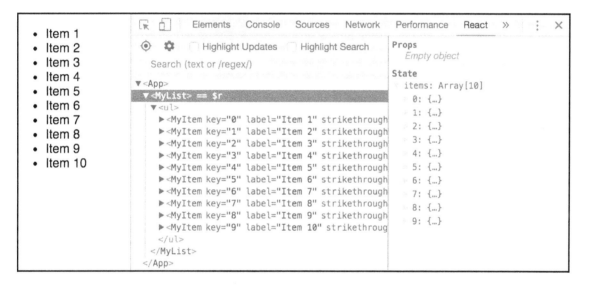

To the right, you can see the state of the selected element. You can actually expand one of the objects in the `items` array and change its property values:

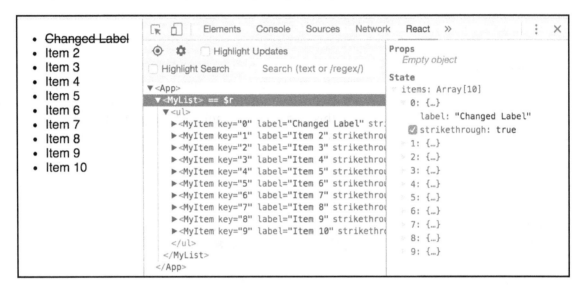

The `label` and `strikethrough` properties of the first object in the `items` array state were changed. This caused the `<MyList>` and the first `<MyItem>` elements to be re-rendered. As expected, the changed state is reflected in the rendered output to the left. This is handy when you need to troubleshoot components that aren't updating their rendered content as they should be. Rather than having to orchestrate some test code within the component, you can simply reach directly into the rendered element's state and manipulate it within the browser.

The one caveat with editing state like this using React Developer Tools is that you can't add or remove items from collections. For example, I can't add a new item to the `items` array, nor can I add a new property to one of the objects in the array. For this, you need to orchestrate your state in the code, as you did in the example prior to this one.

Profiling component performance

Profiling the performance of your React components is made easier by React Developer Tools. It makes it easier to spot updates that cause elements to re-render when no re-render is actually necessary. It also makes it easier to collect the amount of CPU time that a given component spends, and where it spends it during its lifespan.

Although React Developer Tools does not include any memory profile tooling, we'll look at how you can use the existing memory developer tool to specifically profile for React elements.

Removing reconciliation work

Reconciliation is what happens when a React element is rendered. It first computes the virtual DOM tree that will render the element's current state and props. Then, this tree is compared to the existing tree for the element, assuming it has been rendered at least once already. The reason that React does this is because reconciling changes like this in JavaScript, before interacting with the DOM, is more performant. DOM interactions are relatively expensive compared to simple JavaScript code. Additionally, there are a number of common cases that the React reconciler has heuristics for.

React handles all of this for you—you just need to think about writing declarative React components. This doesn't mean that you'll never run into performance issues. Just because reconciliation in JavaScript often performs better than directly manipulating the DOM doesn't mean that it's cheap. So let's put together an application that highlights some potential issues with reconciliation and then let's fix them with the help of React Developer Tools.

We'll create an app that renders groups and members of each group. It'll have controls that change the number of groups and the number of members in each group. Lastly, each rendered group will have a button for adding a new group. Let's start with `index.js`:

```
import React from 'react';
import ReactDOM from 'react-dom';
import './index.css';
import App from './App';
import registerServiceWorker from './registerServiceWorker';

const update = () => {
  ReactDOM.render(<App />, document.getElementById('root'));
};

setInterval(update, 5000);
update();

registerServiceWorker();
```

This is almost like any `index.js` that you would see from `create-react-app`. The difference is that there's an `update()` function that's called in an interval using `setInterval()`. You wouldn't randomly throw an interval timer that re-renders your app every five seconds into your app. I'm adding this here just as a simple means to illustrate repetitive re-rendering and what the reconciliation consequences of this are. You'll likely find similar behavior in a real app where you update components to keep their state fresh—this is an approximation of this behavior.

Next, you have the main `App` component. This is where all of the application state lives, and most of the functionality for that matter. Let's take a look at the file in its entirety, then I'll break it down for you:

```
import React, { Component } from 'react';
import './App.css';
import Group from './Group';

class App extends Component {
  state = {
    groupCount: 10,
    memberCount: 20,
    groups: []
  };

  refreshGroups = (groups, members) => {
    this.setState(state => {
      const groupCount =
        groups === undefined ? state.groupCount : groups;
      const memberCount =
        members === undefined ? state.memberCount : members;
      return {
        ...state,
        groupCount,
        memberCount,
        groups: new Array(groupCount).fill(null).map((g, gi) => ({
          name: 'Group ${gi + 1}',
          members: new Array(memberCount)
            .fill(null)
            .map((m, mi) => ({ name: 'Member ${mi + 1}' }))
        }))
      };
    });
  };

  onGroupCountChange = ({ target: { value } }) => {
    // The + makes value a number.
    this.refreshGroups(+value);
```

```
  };

  onMemberCountChange = ({ target: { value } }) => {
    this.refreshGroups(undefined, +value);
  };

  onAddMemberClick = i => () => {
    this.setState(state => ({
      ...state,
      groups: state.groups.map(
        (v, gi) =>
          i === gi
            ? {
                ...v,
                members: v.members.concat({
                  name: 'Member ${v.members.length + 1}'
                })
              }
            : v
      )
    }));
  };

  componentWillMount() {
    this.refreshGroups();
  }

  render() {
    return (
      <section className="App">
        <div className="Field">
          <label htmlFor="groups">Groups</label>
          <input
            id="groups"
            type="range"
            value={this.state.groupCount}
            min="1"
            max="20"
            onChange={this.onGroupCountChange}
          />
        </div>
        <div className="Field">
          <label htmlFor="members">Members</label>
          <input
            id="members"
            type="range"
            value={this.state.memberCount}
            min="1"
```

```
          max="20"
          onChange={this.onMemberCountChange}
        />
      </div>
      {this.state.groups.map((g, i) => (
        <Group
          key={i}
          name={g.name}
          members={g.members}
          onAddMemberClick={this.onAddMemberClick(i)}
        />
      ))}
    </section>
  );
  }
}

export default App;
```

Let's start with the initial state:

```
state = {
  groupCount: 10,
  memberCount: 20,
  groups: []
};
```

The state that this component manages is as follows:

- `groupCount`: How many groups to render
- `memberCount`: How many members to render in each group
- `groups`: An array of group objects

Each of these values is stored as state because they can be changed. Next, let's look at the `refreshGroups()` function:

```
refreshGroups = (groups, members) => {
  this.setState(state => {
    const groupCount =
      groups === undefined ? state.groupCount : groups;
    const memberCount =
      members === undefined ? state.memberCount : members;
    return {
      ...state,
      groupCount,
      memberCount,
      groups: new Array(groupCount).fill(null).map((g, gi) => ({
```

```
        name: 'Group ${gi + 1}',
        members: new Array(memberCount)
          .fill(null)
          .map((m, mi) => ({ name: 'Member ${mi + 1}' }))
      }))
    };
  });
};
```

Don't worry about the implementation specifics too much here. The purpose of this function is to populate the state as the number of groups and the number of group members change. For example, once called, you'd have state that looks something like:

```
{
  groupCount: 10,
  memberCount: 20,
  groups: [
    {
      Name: 'Group 1',
      Members: [ { name: 'Member 1' }, { name: 'Member 2' } ]
    },
    {
      Name: 'Group 2',
      Members: [ { name: 'Member 1' }, { name: 'Member 2' } ]
    }
  ]
}
```

The reason that this is defined in its own function is because you'll end up calling it in several places. For example, in `componentWillMount()` it is called so that the component has initial state before it's rendered for the first time. Next, let's look at the event handler functions:

```
onGroupCountChange = ({ target: { value } }) => {
  this.refreshGroups(+value);
};

onMemberCountChange = ({ target: { value } }) => {
  this.refreshGroups(undefined, +value);
};

onAddMemberClick = i => () => {
  this.setState(state => ({
    ...state,
    groups: state.groups.map(
      (v, gi) =>
        i === gi
```

```
          ? {
              ...v,
              members: v.members.concat({
                name: 'Member ${v.members.length + 1}'
              })
            }
          : v
      )
    })));
  };
```

These do the following:

- `onGroupCountChange()`: Updates the groups state by calling `refreshGroups()` with the new number of groups
- `onMemberCountChange()`: Updates every member object in the groups state with the new number of members.
- `onAddMemberClick()`: Updates the groups state by adding a new member object at the given index

Finally, let's have a look at the JSX that's rendered by this component:

```
render() {
  return (
    <section className="App">
      <div className="Field">
        <label htmlFor="groups">Groups</label>
        <input
          id="groups"
          type="range"
          value={this.state.groupCount}
          min="1"
          max="20"
          onChange={this.onGroupCountChange}
        />
      </div>
      <div className="Field">
        <label htmlFor="members">Members</label>
        <input
          id="members"
          type="range"
          value={this.state.memberCount}
          min="1"
          max="20"
          onChange={this.onMemberCountChange}
        />
```

```
        </div>
        {this.state.groups.map((g, i) => (
          <Group
            key={i}
            name={g.name}
            members={g.members}
            onAddMemberClick={this.onAddMemberClick(i)}
          />
        ))}
      </section>
    );
  }
}
```

This component renders two slider controls: one that controls the number of groups and one that controls the number of members in each group. Next, the list of groups is rendered. For this, there's a Group component, which looks like this:

```
import React from 'react';
const Group = ({ name, members, onAddMemberClick }) => (
  <section>
    <h4>{name}</h4>
    <button onClick={onAddMemberClick}>Add Member</button>
    <ul>{members.map((m, i) => <li key={i}>{m.name}</li>)}</ul>
  </section>
);

export default Group;
```

This will render the name of the group, followed by a button that adds a new member, and then, by the list of members. When you first load the page, you'll see output that looks like this:

Only a portion of the output is shown here—there are more members in **Group 1** and there are more groups that follow, rendered using the same pattern. Before using any of the controls on this page open up React Developer Tools. Then, look for the **Highlight Updates** checkbox:

Once you've checked this box, your rendered elements will be visually augmented when their state is updated. Recall that you set up the App component to re-render every five seconds. Every time, it's calling setState(), which results in output that looks like this:

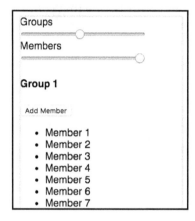

The blue border briefly flashes around the element that's just been updated. Although you can't see everything that <App> renders in this screenshot, the blue border is surrounding all <Group> elements because it's indicating that the <App> component was just updated. If you watch your screen for a few moments, you'll notice that the blue border shows up every 5 seconds. This indicates that even though nothing has changed with the state of your element, it's still performing reconciliation. It's traversing potentially hundreds or thousands of tree nodes to find any differences and make the appropriate DOM updates.

While you can't notice a difference in this app, the cumulative effect of a more complex React application might become a problem. In this specific case, it's a potential problem because of the update frequency.

Let's make an addition to `App` that looks for a shortcut to performing full reconciliation:

```
shouldComponentUpdate(props, state) {
  return (
    this.state.groupCount !== state.groupCount ||
    this.state.memberCount !== state.memberCount
  );
}
```

If a React component class has the `shouldComponentUpdate()` method and it returns false, reconciliation is completely avoided and no re-render takes place. You can see the change immediately in your browser by making sure that the **Highlight Updates** checkbox is checked. If you sit and watch for a few more moments, you'll see that no more blue borders show up.

There are different colors for the update borders. The blue that you're seeing represents infrequent updates. These range all the way to red, depending on the frequency of update. For example, if you slide the groups or members sliders aggressively back and forth, you should be able to produce the red border.

 Note, however, that you can't always avoid reconciliation. What's important is that you macro-optimize for this. For example, the solution that you've just added to the `App` component addresses re-rendering a huge component with lots of children when it clearly isn't necessary. This is valuable compared to micro-optimizing the `Group` component—it's small enough that you don't save much by avoiding reconciliation here.

Your goal should be to keep it high level, and to keep `shouldComponentUpdate()` simple. This is an entry point for bugs to slip into your components. In fact, you've already introduced a bug. Try clicking on one of the **Add Member** buttons for a group—they no longer work. This is because the criteria you're using in `shouldComponentUpdate()` only takes into consideration the `groupCount` and `memberCount` states. It doesn't take into consideration adding new members to groups.

To fix this problem, you have to use the same approach as you have with the `groupCount` and `memberState` states in `shouldComponentUpdate()`. If the total number of members across all groups changes, then you know that your app needs to re-render. Let's make this change in `shouldComponentUpdate()`:

```
shouldComponentUpdate(props, state) {
  const totalMembers = ({ groups }) =>
    groups
      .map(group => group.members.length)
      .reduce((result, m) => result + m);
```

```
    return (
      this.state.groupCount !== state.groupCount ||
      this.state.memberCount !== state.memberCount ||
      totalMembers(this.state) !== totalMembers(state)
    );
  }
```

The `totalMembers()` function takes a component state as an argument and returns the total number of group members. Using this, you can add another condition that uses this function to compare the number of members in the current state to the number of members in the new state:

```
    totalMembers(this.state) !== totalMembers(state)
```

Now if you try clicking on the **Add Member** button again, it will add the member as expected, because the component can detect that something about the state change. Once again, you're trading off the cost of summing the lengths of member arrays and comparing the two, with the cost of performing reconciliation in the React DOM tree.

Finding CPU intensive components

The `shouldComponentUpdate()` life cycle method enables macro-optimization of your component performance. If there's clearly no need to re-render the element, then let's sidestep the reconciliation process entirely. Other times, reconciliation simply cannot be avoided—the element state is changing frequently, and these changes need to be reflected in the DOM for the user to see.

The development version of React 16 has some handy performance tooling built into it. It calls the relevant browser dev tool APIs in order to record relevant metrics while a profile is being recorded. Note that this isn't related to the React Developer Tools browser extension that you installed earlier; this is simply React interacting with the browser when in development mode.

The aim is to produce React-specific timing data so that you don't have to mentally map 20 other browser performance metrics to your component and figure out what they all mean. Everything is there for you.

To demonstrate this functionality, you can use the same code from the previous section with a couple of minor adjustments. First, let's make more members available in each group:

```
state = {
  groupCount: 1,
  memberCount: 200,
  groups: []
};
```

The reason we've increased this number is so that the performance of the app degrades as you fiddle with controls—it's this performance degradation that you want to capture using performance dev tools. Next, let's increase the maximum slider value for the members field:

```
<div className="Field">
  <label htmlFor="members">Members</label>
  <input
    id="members"
    type="range"
    value={this.state.memberCount}
    min="1"
    max="200"
    onChange={this.onMemberCountChange}
  />
</div>
```

That's it. Now when you view this app in your browser, it should look like this:

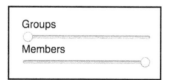

Before changing any of these slider values, make sure that your developer tools pane is open and that the **Performance** tab is selected:

Next, click on the circle icon to the left to start recording a performance profile. The button will change to red and you'll see a status dialog appear, indicating that profiling has started:

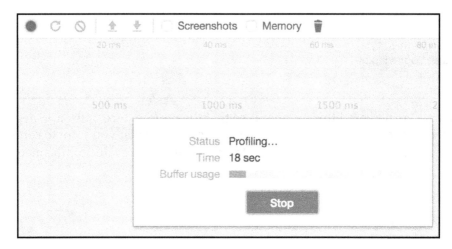

Now that you're recording, slide the **Groups** slider all the way to the right. As you get closer to the right, you might notice some lag in the UI, which is a good thing since this is what you're trying to engineer. Once you reach the right side of the slider, stop the recording by clicking on the red circle that you clicked on to start the recording. You should see something similar to the following:

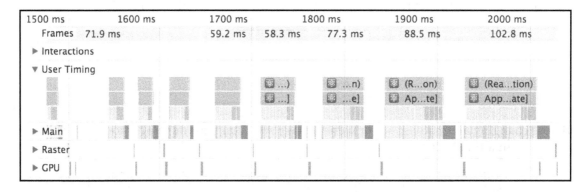

I've expanded the **User Timing** label on the left because this is where all of the React-specific timings are displayed. Time flows from left to right in this graph. The wider something is, the longer it took to happen. You might notice that the performance worsens as you near the right-hand side of the slider (and this might also coincide with the lag you noticed in the slider control).

So, let's explore what some of this data means. We'll look at data on the far right since this is where performance really dropped off:

This label tells you that the **React Tree Reconciliation** took 78 milliseconds to perform. Not terribly slow, but slow enough that it had a tangible impact on user experience. As you move your way down through these labels, you should be able to get a better idea of why the reconciliation process takes as long as it does. Let's look at the next one:

This is interesting: the **App [update]** label is telling you that a state update in the App component took 78 milliseconds. At this point, you know that a state update in App caused the React reconciliation process to take 78 milliseconds. Let's jump down to the next level. At this level, there are two colors. Let's see what the yellow represents:

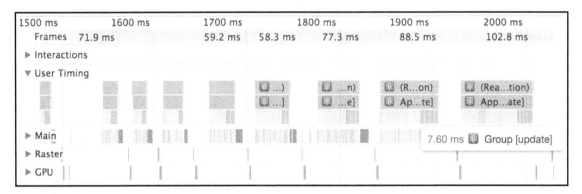

By hovering over one of the yellow slices, you can see that **Group [update]** took 7.7 milliseconds to update a Group component. This is a tiny amount of time that probably can't be improved upon in any meaningful way. However, take a look at the number of yellow slices representing Group updates. All of these slices of single-digit timings add up to a significant portion of the overall reconciliation time. Lastly, let's look at the brown color:

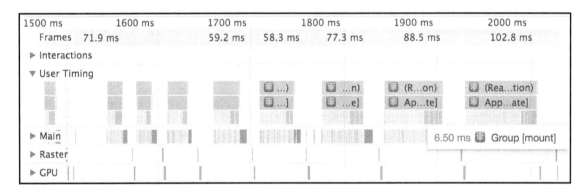

This label, **Group [mount]**, indicates that it took 6.5 milliseconds to mount a new Group component. Once again, this is a small number, but there are several slices of them.

At this point, you've drilled all the way down to the bottom of the component hierarchy to examine what's causing your performance issues. What's the takeaway here? You determined that the bulk of the time taken by React to perform reconciliation is happening in the `Group` component. Each time it renders a `Group` component, it only takes single-digit milliseconds to complete, but there are a lot of groups.

Thanks to the performance graph in the browser developer tools, you now know that there's nothing to gain by changing your code—you're not going to improve on single-digit millisecond times in any meaningful way. In this app, the only way to fix the lag that you felt as you moved the slider toward the right is to somehow reduce the number of elements that get rendered on the page. On the other hand, you might notice that some of these React performance metrics have 50 milliseconds, or hundreds of milliseconds in some cases. You can easily fix your code to provide a better user experience. The key is that you'll never know what actually makes a difference without a performance dev tool like the one you've worked with in this section.

You can often feel the performance issues when you interact with your application as a user. But another way to verify that your components have performance woes is to look at the frame rate that is displayed just above the React metrics in green. It shows you how long frames took to render during the corresponding React code below. This example that you've just built starts off at 40 frames per second when the slider is to the left but ends at 10 frames per second when the slider makes it all the way to the right.

Summary

In this chapter, you learned about React tooling that is available directly through the web browser. The tool of choice here is a Chrome/Firefox extension called React Developer Tools. This extension adds React-specific capabilities to the browsers native developer tools. After you installed the extension, you learned how to select React elements and how to search for React elements by tag name.

Next, you looked at the properties and state values of the selected React component in React Developer Tools. These values are kept up to date automatically, as they're changed by your application. You then learned how to directly manipulate element state directly within the browser. The limitation here being that you can't add or remove values from collections.

Finally, you learned how to profile your React component performance within the browser. This isn't a React Developer Tools feature, but something the develop build of React 16 does automatically. Using profiles like these allows you to make sure that you're addressing the right things when you're experiencing performance issues. The example that you looked at in this chapter showed that there wasn't actually anything wrong with the code—it was a problem of rendering too many elements on the screen at once.

In the next chapter, you'll build a Redux-based React application and use Redux DevTools to instrument the state of your application.

Instrumenting Application State with Redux

9

Redux is the de facto library for managing state in your React applications. On their own, React applications can manage the state of their components using nothing but `setState()`. The challenge with this approach is that there's nothing controlling the ordering of state changes (think about asynchronous calls like HTTP requests).

The aim of this chapter isn't to introduce you to Redux—there are plenty of resources for this, including Packt books and the official Redux documentation. So, if you're new to Redux, you might want to spend 30 minutes familiarizing yourself with the basics of Redux before continuing here. The focus of this chapter is the tooling that you can enable within your web browser. I think that a significant portion of the value of Redux comes from the Redux DevTools browser extension.

In this chapter, you'll learn:

- How to build a basic Redux app (without going into depth on Redux concepts)
- Installing the Redux DevTools Chrome extension
- Selecting Redux actions and examining their contents
- How to use time-travel debugging techniques
- Triggering actions manually to change state
- Exporting application state and importing it later

Building a Redux app

The example application that you'll use in this chapter is a basic book manager. The goal is to have something that has enough functionality to demonstrate different Redux actions, but simple enough that you can learn Redux DevTools without feeling overwhelmed.

The high-level functionality of this application is as follows:

- Renders a list of books that you want to keep track of. Each book displays the title, author, and cover image of the book.
- Allows the user to filter the list by typing in a text input.
- The user can create a new book.
- The user can select a book to view more details.
- Books can be deleted.

Let's spend a few minutes walking through the implementation of this app before you dive into the Redux DevTools extension.

The App component and state

The `App` component is the outer shell of the book manager application. You can think of `App` as the container for every other component that gets rendered. It is responsible for rendering the left-hand side navigation, and for defining the routes of the application so that the appropriate components are mounted and unmounted as the user moves around. Here's what the implementation of `App` looks like:

```
import React, { Component } from 'react';
import { connect } from 'react-redux';
import {
  BrowserRouter as Router,
  Route,
  NavLink
} from 'react-router-dom';
import logo from './logo.svg';
import './App.css';
import Home from './Home';
import NewBook from './NewBook';
import BookDetails from './BookDetails';

class App extends Component {
  render() {
    const { title } = this.props;
```

```
    return (
      <Router>
        <div className="App">
          <header className="App-header">
            <img src={logo} className="App-logo" alt="logo" />
            <h1 className="App-title">{title}</h1>
          </header>
          <section className="Layout">
            <nav>
              <NavLink
                exact
                to="/"
                activeStyle={{ fontWeight: 'bold' }}
              >
                Home
              </NavLink>
              <NavLink to="/new" activeStyle={{ fontWeight: 'bold' }}>
                New Book
              </NavLink>
            </nav>
            <section>
              <Route exact path="/" component={Home} />
              <Route exact path="/new" component={NewBook} />
              <Route
                exact
                path="/book/:title"
                component={BookDetails}
              />
            </section>
          </section>
        </div>
      </Router>
    );
  }
}

const mapState = state => state.app;
const mapDispatch = dispatch => ({});
export default connect(mapState, mapDispatch)(App);
```

The connect() function from the react-redux package is used to connect the App component to the Redux store (where your application state lives). The mapState() and mapDispatch() functions add props to the App component—state values and action dispatcher functions respectively. So far, the App component has only one state value and no action dispatcher functions.

For a more in-depth look at how to connect React components to Redux stores, take a look at this page: https://redux.js.org/basics/usage-with-react.

Let's take a look at the app() reducer function next:

```
const initialState = {
  title: 'Book Manager'
};

const app = (state = initialState, action) => {
  switch (action.type) {
    default:
      return state;
  }
};

export default app;
```

There isn't much to the state used by App except a title. In fact, this title never changes. The reducer function simply returns the state that's passed to it. You don't actually need a switch statement here because there are no actions to handle. However, the title state is likely something that will change based on actions—you just don't know yet. It's never a bad idea to set up reducer functions like this so that you can connect a component to the Redux store, and so that once you identify an action that should cause a state change, you have a reducer function ready to handle it.

The Home component and state

The `Home` component is the first component that is rendered as a child component of `App`. The route for `Home` is `/`, and this is where the filter text input and book list are rendered. Here is what the user will see when they first load the app:

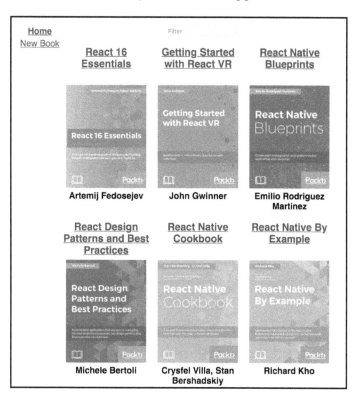

To the left, you have the two navigation links that are rendered by the `App` component. To the right of these links you have the filter text input, followed by the list of books—React books no less. Now, let's take a look at the `Home` component implementation:

```
import React, { Component } from 'react';
import { connect } from 'react-redux';

import { fetchBooks } from '../api';
import Book from './Book';
import Loading from './Loading';
import './Home.css';

class Home extends Component {
```

```
componentWillMount() {
  this.props.fetchBooks();
}

render() {
  const {
    loading,
    books,
    filterValue,
    onFilterChange
  } = this.props;
  return (
    <Loading loading={loading}>
      <section>
        <input
          placeholder="Filter"
          onChange={onFilterChange}
          value={filterValue}
        />
      </section>
      <section className="Books">
        {books
          .filter(
            book =>
              filterValue.length === 0 ||
              new RegExp(filterValue, 'gi').test(book.title)
          )
          .map(book => (
            <Book
              key={book.title}
              title={book.title}
              author={book.author}
              imgURL={book.imgURL}
            />
          ))}
      </section>
    </Loading>
  );
}
}

const mapState = state => state.home;
const mapDispatch = dispatch => ({
  fetchBooks() {
    dispatch({ type: 'FETCHING_BOOKS' });
    fetchBooks().then(books => {
      dispatch({
        type: 'FETCHED_BOOKS',
```

```
          books
      });
    });
  },

  onFilterChange({ target: { value } }) {
    dispatch({ type: 'SET_FILTER_VALUE', filterValue: value });
  }
});

export default connect(mapState, mapDispatch)(Home);
```

The key things to pay attention to here:

- The `componentWillMount()` calls `fetchBooks()` to load book data from the API
- The `Loading` component is used to display loading text while books are being fetched
- The `Home` component defines functions that dispatch actions, something you'll want to look at using Redux DevTools
- The book and filter data come from the Redux store

Here's the reducer function that handles actions and maintains state relevant to this component:

```
const initialState = {
  loading: false,
  books: [],
  filterValue: ''
};

const home = (state = initialState, action) => {
  switch (action.type) {
    case 'FETCHING_BOOKS':
      return {
        ...state,
        loading: true
      };
    case 'FETCHED_BOOKS':
      return {
        ...state,
        loading: false,
        books: action.books
      };

    case 'SET_FILTER_VALUE':
```

```
        return {
          ...state,
          filterValue: action.filterValue
        };

      default:
        return state;
    }
  };

  export default home;
```

If you look at the `initialState` object, you can see that `Home` depends on a `books` array, a `filterValue` string, and a `loading` Boolean. Each of the action cases within the `switch` statement changes part of this state. While it might be a little tricky to decipher what's happening by looking at this reducer code, combined with Redux browser tooling, the picture becomes clear because you can map what you're seeing in the app back to this code.

The NewBook component and state

Under the **Home** link in the left-hand side navigation, there is a **NewBook** link. Clicking on this link will take you to the form that allows you to create a new book. Let's take a look at the `NewBook` component source now:

```
import React, { Component } from 'react';
import { connect } from 'react-redux';

import { createBook } from '../api';
import './NewBook.css';

class NewBook extends Component {
  render() {
    const {
      title,
      author,
      imgURL,
      controlsDisabled,
      onTitleChange,
      onAuthorChange,
      onImageURLChange,
      onCreateBook
    } = this.props;

    return (
      <section className="NewBook">
```

```
          <label>
            Title:
            <input
              autoFocus
              onChange={onTitleChange}
              value={title}
              disabled={controlsDisabled}
            />
          </label>
          <label>
            Author:
            <input
              onChange={onAuthorChange}
              value={author}
              disabled={controlsDisabled}
            />
          </label>
          <label>
            Image URL:
            <input
              onChange={onImageURLChange}
              value={imgURL}
              disabled={controlsDisabled}
            />
          </label>
          <button
            onClick={() => {
              onCreateBook(title, author, imgURL);
            }}
            disabled={controlsDisabled}
          >
            Create
          </button>
        </section>
    );
  }
}
const mapState = state => state.newBook;
const mapDispatch = dispatch => ({
  onTitleChange({ target: { value } }) {
    dispatch({ type: 'SET_NEW_BOOK_TITLE', title: value });
  },

  onAuthorChange({ target: { value } }) {
    dispatch({ type: 'SET_NEW_BOOK_AUTHOR', author: value });
  },

  onImageURLChange({ target: { value } }) {
```

```
      dispatch({ type: 'SET_NEW_BOOK_IMAGE_URL', imgURL: value });
    },

  onCreateBook(title, author, imgURL) {
    dispatch({ type: 'CREATING_BOOK' });
    createBook(title, author, imgURL).then(() => {
      dispatch({ type: 'CREATED_BOOK' });
    });
  }
});

export default connect(mapState, mapDispatch)(NewBook);
```

If you look at the markup that's used to render this component, you'll see that there are three input fields. The values of these fields are passed as props. The connection to the Redux store is actually where these props come from. As their state changes, the NewBook component is re-rendered.

The dispatch functions that are mapped to this component are responsible for dispatching actions that maintain the state of this component. Their responsibilities are as follows:

- onTitleChange(): Dispatches the SET_NEW_BOOK_TITLE action along with the new title state
- onAuthorChange(): Dispatches the SET_NEW_BOOK_AUTHOR action along with the new author state
- onImageURLChange(): Dispatches the SET_NEW_BOOK_IMAGE_URL action along with the new imgURL state
- onCreateBook(): Dispatches the CREATING_BOOK action then dispatches the CREATED_BOOK action when the createBook() API call returns

Don't worry if it's not clear how all of these actions result in high-level application behavior. This is why you're going to install Redux DevTools shortly, so that you can understand what's happening with your application state as it changes.

Here's the reducer function that handles these actions:

```
const initialState = {
  title: '',
  author: '',
  imgURL: '',
  controlsDisabled: false
};

const newBook = (state = initialState, action) => {
```

```
switch (action.type) {
  case 'SET_NEW_BOOK_TITLE':
    return {
      ...state,
      title: action.title
    };
  case 'SET_NEW_BOOK_AUTHOR':
    return {
      ...state,
      author: action.author
    };
  case 'SET_NEW_BOOK_IMAGE_URL':
    return {
      ...state,
      imgURL: action.imgURL
    };
  case 'CREATING_BOOK':
    return {
      ...state,
      controlsDisabled: true
    };
  case 'CREATED_BOOK':
    return initialState;
  default:
    return state;
  }
};

export default newBook;
```

Finally, here's what the new book form looks like when rendered:

When you fill out these fields and click on the **Create** button, the new book will be created by the mock API and you'll be taken back to the **Home** page, where the new book should be listed.

The API abstraction

For this application, I'm using a simple API abstraction. In Redux apps, you should be able to have your asynchronous functionality—API or otherwise—encapsulated in its own module or package. Here's what the api.js module looks like, with some of the mock data redacted for brevity:

```
const LATENCY = 1000;

const BOOKS = [
  {
    title: 'React 16 Essentials',
    author: 'Artemij Fedosejev',
    imgURL: 'big long url...'
  },
  ...
];

export const fetchBooks = () =>
  new Promise(resolve => {
    setTimeout(() => {
      resolve(BOOKS);
    }, LATENCY);
  });

export const createBook = (title, author, imgURL) =>
  new Promise(resolve => {
    setTimeout(() => {
      BOOKS.push({ title, author, imgURL });
      resolve();
    }, LATENCY);
  });

export const fetchBook = title =>
  new Promise(resolve => {
    setTimeout(() => {
      resolve(BOOKS.find(book => book.title === title));
    }, LATENCY);
  });

export const deleteBook = title =>
  new Promise(resolve => {
    setTimeout(() => {
      BOOKS.splice(BOOKS.findIndex(b => b.title === title), 1);
      resolve();
    }, LATENCY);
  });
```

To get started with building your Redux app, this is all you need. The important thing to note here is that each of these API functions returns a `Promise` object. For good measure, I'm adding some simulated latency because this more closely resembles a real API. Something you don't want to do with your API abstractions is have them return regular values—like objects or arrays. If they're going to be asynchronous when interacting with a real API, make sure that the initial mocks are asynchronous as well. Otherwise, this is exceedingly difficult to correct.

Putting it all together

Let's quickly look at the source files that bring everything together to give you a sense of completeness. Let's start with `index.js`:

```
import React from 'react';
import ReactDOM from 'react-dom';
import './index.css';
import Root from './components/Root';
import registerServiceWorker from './registerServiceWorker';

ReactDOM.render(<Root />, document.getElementById('root'));
registerServiceWorker();
```

This looks just like most `index.js` files in `create-react-app` that you've worked with so far in this book. Instead of rendering an `App` component, it's rendering a `Root` component. Let's look at this next:

```
import React from 'react';
import { Provider } from 'react-redux';
import App from './App';
import store from '../store';

const Root = () => (
  <Provider store={store}>
    <App />
  </Provider>
);

export default Root;
```

The job of `Root` is to wrap the `App` component with a `Provider` component from `react-redux`. This component takes a `store` prop, which is how you're able to ensure that connected components have access to Redux store data.

Let's take a look at the `store` prop next:

```
import { createStore } from 'redux';
import reducers from './reducers';

export default createStore(
  reducers,
  window.__REDUX_DEVTOOLS_EXTENSION__ &&
    window.__REDUX_DEVTOOLS_EXTENSION__()
);
```

Redux has a `createStore()` function that builds a store for your React app. The first argument is the reducer function that handles actions and returns the new state of the store. The second argument is an enhancer function that can respond to changes in store state. In this case, you want to check if the Redux DevTools browser extension is installed and if it is, then connect it to your store. Without this step, you won't be able to use browser tooling with your Redux app.

We're almost done. Let's look at the `reducers/index.js` file that combines your reducer functions into one function:

```
import { combineReducers } from 'redux';
import app from './app';
import home from './home';
import newBook from './newBook';
import bookDetails from './bookDetails';

const reducers = combineReducers({
  app,
  home,
  newBook,
  bookDetails
});

export default reducers;
```

Redux has only one store. In order to subdivide your store into slices of state that map to the concepts of your application, you name the individual reducer functions that handle the various slices of state and pass them to `combineReducers()`. With this app, your store has the following slices of state that can be mapped to components:

- app
- home
- newBook
- bookDetails

Now that you've seen how this app is put together and how it works, it's time to start instrumenting it with the Redux DevTools browser extension.

Installing Redux DevTools

Installing the Redux DevTools browser extension follows a process similar to the one used to install the React Developer Tools extension. The first step is to open the Chrome Web Store and search for `redux`:

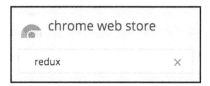

The extension that you're looking for will likely be the first result:

Go ahead and click on the **Add To Chrome** button. You'll then see a dialog that asks for your permission to install the extension after showing you what it can change:

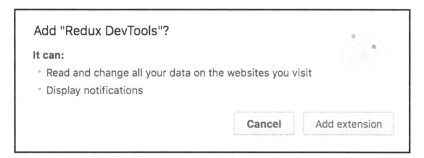

After you click on the **Add extension** button, you'll see a notification that the extension has been installed:

Just like the React Developer Tools extension, the Redux DevTools icon will remain disabled until you open a page that is running Redux and has added support for the tool. Recall that you explicitly added support for this tool in the book manager app with the following code:

```
export default createStore(
  reducers,
  window.__REDUX_DEVTOOLS_EXTENSION__ &&
    window.__REDUX_DEVTOOLS_EXTENSION__()
);
```

Now let's fire up the book manager app and make sure that you can use the extension with it. After running `npm start` and waiting for the UI to open and load in a browser tab, the React and Redux developer tool icons should both be enabled:

Next, open up the developer tools browser pane. You can access the Redux DevTools the same way that you would access the React Developer Tools:

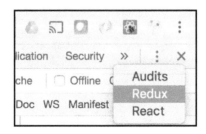

When you select the Redux tool, you should see something similar to this:

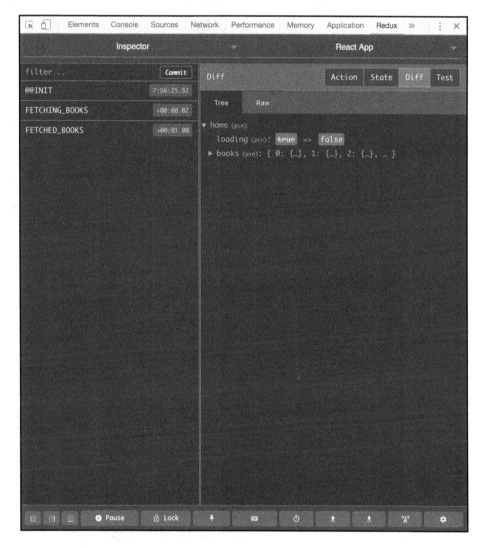

The left pane in the Redux DevTools has the most important data—the actions in your application. As reflected here, three actions have been dispatched by your book manager app, so you know that everything's working!

Selecting and examining actions

The actions displayed on the left-hand side pane of Redux DevTools are listed chronologically, based on when they were dispatched. Any action can be selected, and by doing so, you can use the right-hand side pane to examine different aspects of the application state and of the action itself. In this section, you'll learn how to look deeper into how Redux actions drive your application.

Action data

By selecting an action, you can view the data that's dispatched as part of the action. But first, let's generate some actions. Once the app loads, the FETCHING_BOOKS and FETCHED_BOOKS actions are dispatched. Click on the **React Native Blueprints** link, which loads the book data and takes you to the book details page. This results in two new actions being dispatched: FETCHING_BOOK and FETCHED_BOOK. The rendered React content should look like this:

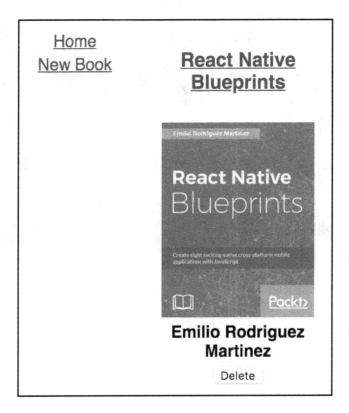

The list of actions in Redux DevTools should look like this:

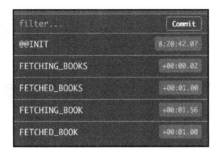

The @@INIT action is dispatched automatically by Redux and is always the first action. Typically, you don't need to worry about this action unless you need to know what the state of your application looked like before dispatching and actions—we'll cover this in the following section.

For now, let's select the FETCHING_BOOKS action. Then, in the right-hand side pane, select the **Action** toggle button to see action data. You should see something that looks like this:

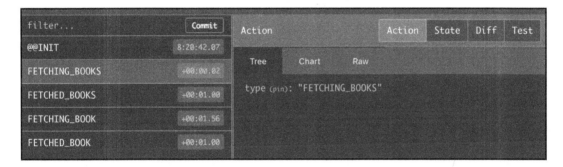

The tree view of the action is selected by default. You can see here that the action data has a single property called type and its value is the name of the action. This tells you that the reducer should know what to do with this action and that it doesn't need any additional data.

Let's select the `FETCHED_BOOKS` action now and see what the action data looks like:

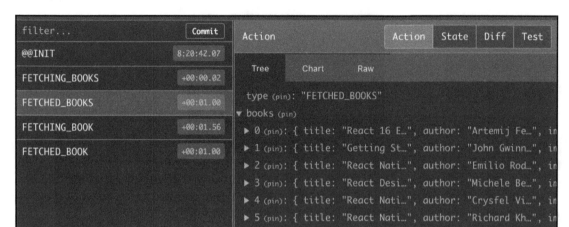

Once again, you have the `type` property with the name of the action. This time, you also have a `books` property with an array of books. This action is dispatched in response to API data resolving and how book data makes its way into the store—its carried in by an action.

By looking at action data, you can compare what's actually dispatched versus what you're seeing in your application state. The only way to change application state is by dispatching actions with new state. Next, let's look at how individual actions change the state of the application.

Action state trees and charts

In the previous section, you saw how to use Redux DevTools to select specific actions to view their data. Actions and the data that they carry lead to changes in application state. When you select an action, you can view the effect that the action has on the overall application state.

Let's select the `FETCHING_BOOK` action and then select the **State** toggle button in the right-hand side pane:

This **Tree** view shows you the entire state of the application after the FETCHING_BOOK action is dispatched. The bookDetails state is expanded here so that you can see the effect the action has on the state. In this case it's the loading value—which is now true.

Let's select the **Chart** view of this action now:

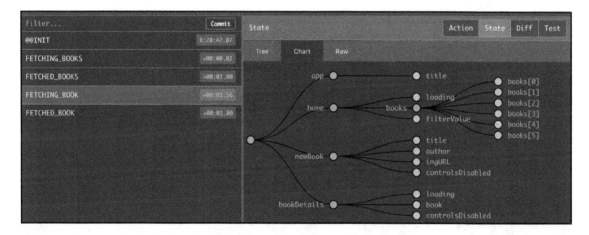

I happen to like the **Chart** view better than the **Tree** view for visualizing the entire state of the application. At the far left of the chart you have the root state. To the right of this, you have the main slices of application state—app, home, newBook, and bookDetails. As you move further and further right, you're drilling down into the specific state of components in your app. As you can see here, the deepest level is the individual books within the books array, which is part of the home state.

The FETCHING_BOOK action is still selected, which means that this chart is a reflection of the application state after reducers have responded to this action. This action changes the loading state within bookDetails. If you move your mouse pointer over the state label, you'll see its value:

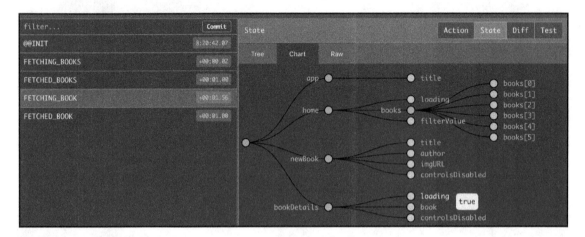

Now let's select the FETCHED_BOOK action. This action is dispatched when the book detail data is resolved from the API call that is made to get it:

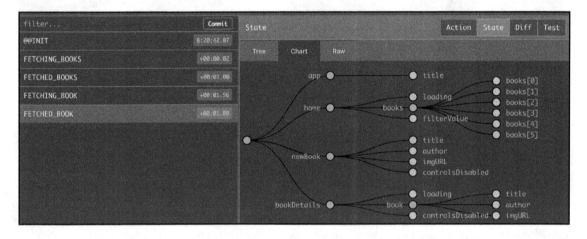

If you keep the **Chart** view activated while switching to a different action, you'll notice that the chart actually animates the changes in state. It looks cool, no doubt, but it also calls your attention to the values that actually changes so that they're easier to see. In this example, if you look at the `book` object under `bookDetails`, you'll see that it now has new properties. You can move your mouse pointer over each of them to reveal their value. You can also check the `loading` value—it should be back to `false`.

Action state diffs

Another way to view action data in Redux DevTools is to look at the state diff that results from dispatching the action. Instead of trying to glean the changes in state by looking at the entire state tree, this view only shows you what changed.

Let's try adding a new book to generate some actions. I'm going to add the book you're reading right now. First, I'll paste in the title of the book that generates a change event on the input element, which in turn dispatches a `SET_NEW_BOOK_TITLE` action. If you select the action, you should see the following:

The `title` value of the `newBook` state went from an empty string to the value that was pasted into the title text input. Rather than having to hunt this change down, it is clearly marked for you to see, with all irrelevant state data hidden from view.

Next, let's paste in the author and select the `SET_NEW_BOOK_AUTHOR` action:

Once again, only the author value is shown here because it's the only value that changed as a result of dispatching SET_NEW_BOOK_AUTHOR. Here's the final form field—the image URL:

By using the **Diff** view of actions, you only see data that has changed as a result of the action. If this doesn't give you enough perspective, you can always jump to the **State** view so that you can see the state of the entire application.

Let's create the new book by clicking the **Create** button. This will dispatch two actions: CREATING_BOOK and CREATED_BOOK. First, let's look at CREATING_BOOK:

This action is dispatched before the API call to *create the book* is made. This gives your React component an opportunity to handle the asynchronous nature of the user interaction. In this case, you don't want the user to be able to interact with any form controls while the request is pending. As you can see by looking at this diff, the controlsDisabled value is now false, which the React component can use to disable any form controls.

Lastly, let's look at the `CREATED_BOOK` action:

The `title`, `author`, and `imgURL` values are set to empty strings, which resets the form field values. The form fields are also re-enabled by setting `controlsDisabled` to `false`.

Time travel debugging

One requirement of reducer functions in Redux is that they're pure; that is, they only return new data as opposed to mutating existing data. One consequence of this is that it enables time travel debugging. Because nothing ever changes, you can move the state of your application forward, backward, or to an arbitrary point in time. The Redux DevTools make this easy to do.

To see time travel debugging in action, let's type some filter text into the filter input box:

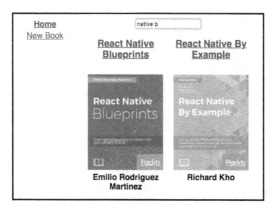

Looking at the actions in Redux DevTools, you should see something along these lines:

I've selected the last `SET_FILTER_VALUE` action that was dispatched. The `filterValue` value should be `native b`, which reflects the titles that are currently displayed. Now, let's travel back to two actions ago. To do this, move your mouse pointer over the action that's two positions behind the currently selected action. Click on the **Jump** button, and the state of the application will be changed to the state when this `SET_FILTER_VALUE` was dispatched:

You can see that `filterValue` has changed from `native b` to `native`. You've effectively undone the last two keystrokes, updating the state and the UI accordingly:

To bring the application state back to the current time, follow the same process but in reverse. Click on **Jump** on the most recent state.

Manually triggering actions

The ability to manually trigger actions during development of a Redux application can be helpful. For instance, you might have components ready, but you're unsure of how the user interaction will work or you just need to troubleshoot something that should be working but isn't. You can use Redux DevTools to manually trigger actions by clicking on the button with the keyboard icon, near the bottom of the pane:

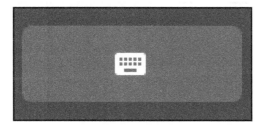

This will display a text input where you can enter the action payload. For example, I've navigated to the book detail page for **React Native By Example**:

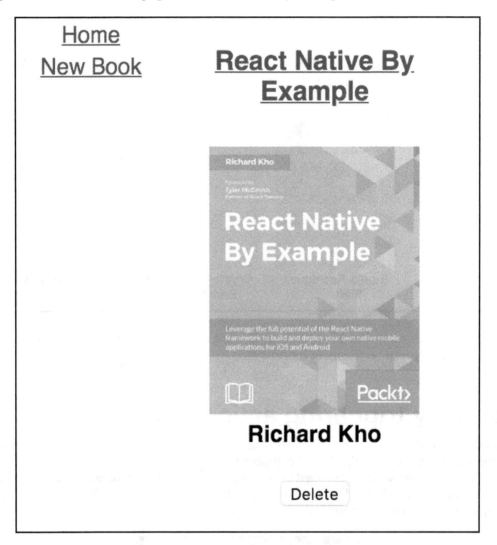

Instead of clicking on the **Delete** button, I only want to see what happens regarding the state of the application, without triggering DOM events or API calls. To do this, I can click on the keyboard button in Redux DevTools, which allows me to manually enter an action and dispatch it. For example, here is how I would dispatch the DELETING_BOOK action:

This results in the action being dispatched and consequently, the UI is updated. Here's the DELETING_BOOK action:

To set controlsDisabled back to false, you can dispatch the DELETED_BOOK action:

Exporting and importing state

As your Redux applications grow in size and complexity, the size and complexity of your state trees will grow in tandem. Because of this, there will be times when playing around with individual actions and to get your app into a specific state could be too cumbersome to perform manually over and over again.

Using Redux DevTools, you can export the current state of the application. Then, when you're troubleshooting later on and you need a specific state as a starting point, you can load it directly, rather than manually recreate it.

Let's try exporting the application state. First, navigate to the details page for **React 16 Essentials**:

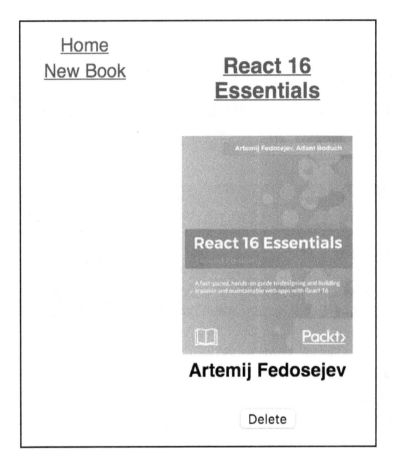

To export the current state using Redux DevTools, click on the button with the down arrow:

Then, you can use the up arrow to import the state. But before you do that, navigate to a different book title, such as **Getting Started with React VR**:

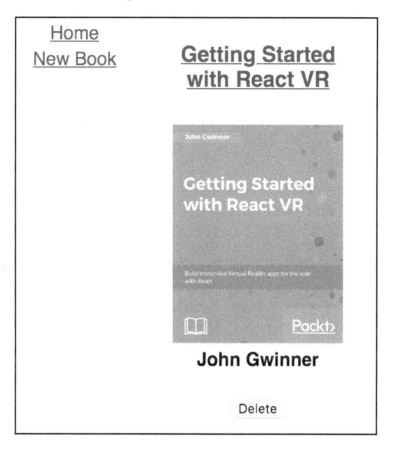

Now, you can use the upload button in the Redux DevTools pane:

Since you're already on the book details page, loading this state will replace the state values that are rendered by components on this page:

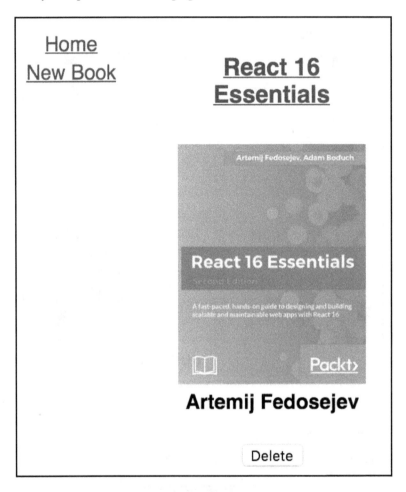

Now you know how to restore the state of your Redux store to any given point that you've exported and saved locally. The idea is to avoid having to remember and perform the correction actions in the correct order to arrive at a particular state. This is error-prone and exporting the exact state that's needed obviates the whole process.

Summary

In this chapter, you put together a simple book manager Redux app. With the app in place, you then learned how to install the Redux DevTools browser extension in Chrome. From there, you learned how to view and select actions.

There are a number of ways to view information about the application once you've selected an action. You can look at the action payload data. You can look at the application state in its entirety. You can look at diffs between the app state and the last dispatched action. These are all different approaches you can use to instrument your Redux applications.

Then, you learned how time travel debugging works in Redux DevTools. Because state changes are immutable in Redux, you can use Redux DevTools to jump around from action to action. This can drastically simplify debugging cycles. Lastly, you learned how to manually dispatch actions and import/export the state of your application.

In the next chapter, you'll learn how to use Gatsby to generate static content from React components.

10
Building and Deploying Static React Sites with Gatsby

Gatsby is a static website generation tool for React developers. In essence, this tool lets you build React components and captures their rendered output to use as the static site content. However, Gatsby takes static site generation to the next level. In particular, it provides mechanisms for sourcing your website data and transforming it into GraphQL that's more easily consumed by React components. Gatsby can handle anything from a single page brochure site to a site that spans hundreds of pages.

Here's what you'll learn in this chapter:

- Why you would want to build a static site using React components
- Building simple Gatsby sites using starters
- Using data from your local filesystem
- Using remote data from Hacker News

Why static React sites?

Before you get started with building static websites using Gatsby, let's set the context with a brief discussion on why you would want to do this. There are three key factors at play here —we'll go over each of them now.

Types of React apps

React has connotations with apps that are very interactive and with lively data that changes a lot. This might be true of some apps, perhaps even most apps, but there are still cases where the user is looking at static data—information that doesn't change or changes very infrequently.

Consider a blog. The typical flow is for an author to publish some content and then that content is served to anyone who visits the site, who can then view the content. The common case is that once the content is published, it stays the same, or, it stays static. The uncommon case is that the author makes updates to their post, but even then, this is an infrequent action. Now, think about your typical blog publishing platform. Every time a reader visits a page on your blog, database queries are executed, content has to be assembled, and so on. Ask yourself, is there really any point in issuing all of these queries if the results are going to be the same every time?

Let's look at another example. You have an enterprise-style app—a large app with lots of data and lots of features. One part of the app is focused on user interactivity—adding/changing data and interacting with near real-time data. Another part of the app generates reporting—reports based on database queries and charts based on historical snapshots of data. The latter part of this enterprise application doesn't appear to interact with data that changes frequently, or at all. Perhaps, the app could benefit by being split into two apps: one that handles user interactions with lively data, and another one that generates static content that doesn't change frequently, or at all.

You might be building an app or part of a larger app where you have mostly static data. If so, you could probably use a tool like Gatsby to generate statically rendered content. But why do this? What's the benefit?

Better user experience

The most compelling reason for building a static version of your React components is to provide a better experience for your users. The key metric here is the overall performance improvements. Instead of having to touch various API endpoints and handle all of the asynchronous aspects of providing data to your React components, everything is loaded upfront.

Another less obvious user experience improvement with statically built React content is that since there are fewer moving parts, there's less chance of the site breaking, leading to user frustration. For example, if your React components don't have to reach out over the network to fetch data, this failure vector is removed entirely from your site.

Efficient resource usage

Components that are statically compiled by Gatsby know how to make efficient use of the GraphQL resources that they consume. One of the great things about GraphQL is that it's easy for tools to parse and generate efficient code at compile time. If you want a more in-depth introduction to GraphQL before continuing with Gatsby, a good one can be found here: `http://graphql.org/learn/`.

Another place that static Gatsby React apps help reduce resource consumption is in the backend. These apps aren't constantly hitting API endpoints that return the same response every single time. This is time that the same API and database could be spent servicing requests that actually need dynamic data or are generating new data.

Building your first Gatsby site

The first step to using Gatsby is to install the command-line tool globally:

```
npm install gatsby-cli -g
```

Now you can run the command-line tool to generate your Gatsby project, not unlike how `create-react-app` works. The `gatsby` command takes two arguments:

- The name of the new project
- The URL of the Gatsby starter repository

The project name is basically the name of the folder that's created to hold all of your project files. A Gatsby starter is kind of like a template that makes it easier for you to get rolling, especially if you're learning. If you don't pass a starter, the default starter is used:

```
gatsby new your-first-gatsby-site
```

Running the above command would be the same as running:

```
gatsby new your-first-gatsby-site
https://github.com/gatsbyjs/gatsby-starter-default
```

In both cases, the starter repository is cloned into the `your-first-gatsby-site` directory and then dependencies are installed for you. If all goes well, you should see the console output that looks similar to this:

```
info Creating new site from git:
https://github.com/gatsbyjs/gatsby-starter-default.git
Cloning into 'your-first-gatsby-site'...
```

```
success Created starter directory layout
info Installing packages...
added 1540 packages from 888 contributors in 29.528s
```

Now you can change into the `your-first-gatsby-site` directory and start the development server:

```
cd your-first-gatsby-site
gatsby develop
```

This starts the Gatsby development server within your project. Once again, this is similar to how `create-react-app` works—there's zero configuration to deal with and Webpack is setup to just work. After starting the development server, you should see output on the console that looks like this:

```
success delete html and css files from previous builds - 0.007 s
success open and validate gatsby-config.js - 0.004 s
success copy gatsby files - 0.014 s
success onPreBootstrap - 0.011 s
success source and transform nodes - 0.022 s
success building schema - 0.070 s
success createLayouts - 0.020 s
success createPages - 0.000 s
success createPagesStatefully - 0.014 s
success onPreExtractQueries - 0.000 s
success update schema - 0.044 s
success extract queries from components - 0.042 s
success run graphql queries - 0.024 s
success write out page data - 0.003 s
success write out redirect data - 0.001 s
success onPostBootstrap - 0.001 s
info bootstrap finished - 1.901 s
DONE  Compiled successfully in 3307ms
```

You can now view `gatsby-starter-default` in the browser by navigating to `http://localhost:8000/`.

View GraphiQL, an in-browser IDE, to explore your site's data and schema `http://localhost:8000/___graphql`.

Note that the development build is not optimized. To create a production build, use `gatsby build`:

```
WAIT  Compiling...
DONE  Compiled successfully in 94ms
```

If you visit `http://localhost:8000/` in your web browser, you should see the default content:

The default starter creates multiple pages so that you can see how to link your pages together. If you click on the **Go to page 2** link, you'll be taken to the next page of the site, which looks like this:

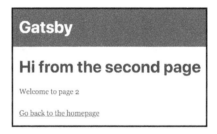

Here's what the structure of your default Gatsby starter project looks like:

```
├──── LICENSE
├──── README.md
├──── gatsby-browser.js
├──── gatsby-config.js
├──── gatsby-node.js
├──── gatsby-ssr.js
├──── package-lock.json
├──── package.json
├──── public
│     ├──── index.html
│     ├──── render-page.js.map
│     └──── static
└──── src
      ├──── components
      │     └──── Header
```

```
|               └──── index.js
├──── layouts
|       ├──── index.css
|       └──── index.js
└──── pages
        ├──── 404.js
        ├──── index.js
        └──── page-2.js
```

For basic site design and editing, you'll mostly be concerned with files and directories under src. Let's take a look at what you have to work with here, starting with the Header component:

```
import React from 'react'
import Link from 'gatsby-link'

const Header = () => (
  <div
    style={{
      background: 'rebeccapurple',
      marginBottom: '1.45rem',
    }}
  >
    <div
      style={{
        margin: '0 auto',
        maxWidth: 960,
        padding: '1.45rem 1.0875rem',
      }}
    >
      <h1 style={{ margin: 0 }}>
        <Link
          to="/"
          style={{
            color: 'white',
            textDecoration: 'none',
          }}
        >
          Gatsby
        </Link>
      </h1>
    </div>
  </div>
)

export default Header
```

This component defines the purple header section. The title is static for now, it links to the home page, and defines some inline styles. Next, let's look at the `layouts/index.js` file:

```
import React from 'react'
import PropTypes from 'prop-types'
import Helmet from 'react-helmet'

import Header from '../components/Header'
import './index.css'

const TemplateWrapper = ({ children }) => (
  <div>
    <Helmet
      title="Gatsby Default Starter"
      meta={[
        { name: 'description', content: 'Sample' },
        { name: 'keywords', content: 'sample, something' },
      ]}
    />
    <Header />
    <div
      style={{
        margin: '0 auto',
        maxWidth: 960,
        padding: '0px 1.0875rem 1.45rem',
        paddingTop: 0,
      }}
    >
      {children()}
    </div>
  </div>
)

TemplateWrapper.propTypes = {
  children: PropTypes.func,
}

export default TemplateWrapper
```

This module exports a `TemplateWrapper` component. The job of this component is to define the layout for the site. Like other container components that you might have implemented, this one is rendered on every page of the site. It's similar to what you would do with `react-router`, except with Gatsby, the routing is handled for you. For example, the route that handles the link that points to `page-2` is created automatically by Gatsby. Likewise, Gatsby automatically handles this layout module for you by making sure that it's rendered by every page on the site. All you have to do is make sure that it looks the way you want it to and that the `children()` function is rendered. For now, you can just leave it as is.

You'll notice, too, that the layout module also imports a stylesheet that contains styles pertinent to the layout of the site.

Let's look at the page components now, starting with `index.js`:

```
import React from 'react'
import Link from 'gatsby-link'

const IndexPage = () => (
  <div>
    <h1>Hi people</h1>
    <p>Welcome to your new Gatsby site.</p>
    <p>Now go build something great.</p>
    <Link to="/page-2/">Go to page 2</Link>
  </div>
)

export default IndexPage
```

Just like plain HTML sites have an `index.html` file, it's important that static Gatsby sites have an `index.js` page that exports the content to render on the home page. The `IndexPage` component that's defined here renders some basic HTML, including a link to `page-2`. Let's look at `page-2.js` next:

```
import React from 'react'
import Link from 'gatsby-link'

const SecondPage = () => (
  <div>
    <h1>Hi from the second page</h1>
    <p>Welcome to page 2</p>
    <Link to="/">Go back to the homepage</Link>
  </div>
)
export default SecondPage
```

This page looks very similar to the home page. The link that's rendered here takes the user back to the home page.

This was just a basic introduction to get you rolling with Gatsby. You didn't use any data sources to generate content; you'll do just that in the following section.

Adding local filesystem data

In the previous section, you saw how to get a basic Gatsby website up and running. This website wasn't very interesting because there was no data to drive it. For example, the data that drives a blog is the blog entry content stored in a database—the blog framework that renders the post lists and posts themselves use this data to render markup.

You can do the same thing with Gatsby but in a more sophisticated way. First, the markup (or in this case, React components) is statically built and bundled once. These builds are then served to users without having to query a database or API. Second, the plugin architecture used by Gatsby means that you're not restricted to only one source of data and that different sources are often combined. Lastly, GraphQL is the querying abstraction that sits on top of all of these things and delivers data to your React components.

To get started, you need a data source to drive the content of your website. We'll keep things simple for now and use a local JSON file as the source. To do so, you need to install the `gatsby-source-filesystem` plugin:

```
npm install --save gatsby-source-filesystem
```

Once this package is installed, you can add it to your project by editing your `gatsby-config.js` file:

```
plugins: [
  // Other plugins...
  {
    resolve: 'gatsby-source-filesystem',
    options: {
      name: 'data',
      path: '${__dirname}/src/data/',
    },
  },
]
```

The `name` option tells the GraphQL backend how to organize the query result. In this case, everything will be under a `data` property. The path option restricts which files are readable. The path used in this example is `src/data`—feel free to throw a file into that directory so that it's queryable.

At this point, you can go ahead and start up the Gatsby development server. The GraphiQL utility is accessible at `http://localhost:8000/___graphql`. When developing Gatsby websites, you will utilize this tool often as it allows you to create ad hoc GraphQL queries and execute them on the fly. When you first load this interface, you'll see something like this:

The left panel is where you write your GraphQL queries, clicking on the Play button above executes the query, and the panel to the right displays the query results. The docs link in the top-right is a useful way to explore the available GraphQL types that Gatsby creates for you. Additionally, the query editor pane to the right will autocomplete as you type to help make building queries easier.

Let's execute your first query that lists information about files on the filesystem. Remember that you need at least one file in `src/data` in order to have your query return any results. Here is how to query the name, extension, and the size of files in your data directory:

```
GraphiQL   ▶    Prettify   History                                          ⟨ Docs

 1▾ {                                    ▾ {
 2▾    allFile {                         ▾    "data": {
 3▾      edges {                         ▾      "allFile": {
 4▾        node {                        ▾        "edges": [
 5           name,                       ▾          {
 6           ext,                        ▾            "node": {
 7           prettySize                               "name": "articles",
 8        }                                            "ext": ".json",
 9      }                                              "prettySize": "323 B"
10    }                                              }
11  }.                                             }
                                                 ]
                                               }
                                             }
                                           }
```

As you can see, specific node fields are specified in the query. The result in the right panel shows that you get the exact fields that you ask for. Part of GraphQLs appeal is that you can create arbitrarily nested and complex queries that span multiple backend data sources. However, delving into the specifics of GraphQL go way beyond the scope of this book. The Gatsby home page (`https://www.gatsbyjs.org/`) has some great resources on GraphQL, including links to other GraphQL tutorials and documentation.

The takeaway here is that the `gatsby-source-filesystem` data source plugin did all of the heavy GraphQL lifting for you. It generates the entire schema for you, which means that once you have the plugin installed, you can start the development server and experiment with autocomplete and documentation right away.

Moving forward with the example, you probably don't have any need to render local file data in your UI. So let's create a `articles.json` file that has some JSON content:

```
[
    { "topic": "global", "title": "Global Article 1" },
    { "topic": "global", "title": "Global Article 2" },
    { "topic": "local", "title": "Local Article 1" },
    { "topic": "local", "title": "Local Article 2" },
    { "topic": "sports", "title": "Sports Article 1" },
    { "topic": "sports", "title": "Sports Article 2" }
]
```

This JSON structure is an array of article objects with `topic` and `title` properties. This is the data that you want to query with GraphQL. To do so, you need to install another Gatsby plugin:

```
npm install --save gatsby-transformer-json
```

The `gatsby-transformer-json` plugin is from another category of Gatsby plugins—transformers. Source plugins are responsible from feeding data into Gatsby, while transformers are responsible for making the data queryable via GraphQL. Just like any plugin you want to use, you need to add it to your project config:

```
plugins: [
  // Other plugins...
  'gatsby-transformer-json',
],
```

Now that you have a file with JSON content in your data directory and the `gatsby-transformer-json` plugin installed and enabled, you can go back to GraphiQL and query for JSON content:

The `gatsby-transformer-json` plugin makes the `allArticlesJson` query possible because it defines the GraphQL schema for you, based on the JSON data found in the data source. Under `node`, you can ask for specific properties, as you would with any other GraphQL query. In the results, you get all of the JSON data that your query asked for.

In this example, let's assume that you want three separate pages for listing articles, organized by topic. You need a way to filter the nodes that are returned by the query. You can add filters directly into your GraphQL syntax. For example, to find only global articles, you do execute the following query:

This time a filter argument is passed to the `allArticlesJson` query. Here, the query is asking for nodes with a topic value of global. Sure enough, the articles with a global topic are returned in the result.

The GraphiQL utility allows you to design a GraphQL query that can then be used by your React component. Once you have a query that's returning the correct results, you can simply copy it into your component. This last query returns global articles, so you can use it with the component used for the `pages/global.js` page:

```
import React from 'react'
import Link from 'gatsby-link'

export default ({ data: { allArticlesJson: { edges } } }) => (
  <div>
    <h1>Global Articles</h1>
    <Link to="/">Home</Link>
    <ul>
```

```
        {edges.map((({ node: { title } }) => (
          <li key={title}>{title}</li>
        )))}
      </ul>
    </div>
  )

  export const query = graphql'
    query GlobalArticles {
      allArticlesJson(filter: { topic: { eq: "global" } }) {
        edges {
          node {
            topic
            title
          }
        }
      }
    }
  '
```

There are two things to pay attention to in this module. First, look at the argument passed to the component and notice how it matches the result data that you saw in GraphiQL. This data is then used to render the list of global article titles. Next, notice the query export string. During build time, Gatsby will find this string and execute the appropriate GraphQL query so that your component has a static snapshot of the results.

Given that you now know how to filter for global articles, you can now update the filter for the pages/local.js page:

```
import React from 'react'
import Link from 'gatsby-link'

export default ({ data: { allArticlesJson: { edges } } }) => (
  <div>
    <h1>Local Articles</h1>
    <Link to="/">Home</Link>
    <ul>
      {edges.map((({ node: { title } }) => (
        <li key={title}>{title}</li>
      )))}
    </ul>
  </div>
)
export const query = graphql'
  query LocalArticles {
    allArticlesJson(filter: { topic: { eq: "local" } }) {
      edges {
```

```
        node {
          topic
          title
        }
      }
    }
  }
'
```

And here's what the `pages/sports.js` page looks like:

```
import React from 'react'
import Link from 'gatsby-link'

export default ({ data: { allArticlesJson: { edges } } }) => (
  <div>
    <h1>Sports Articles</h1>
    <Link to="/">Home</Link>
    <ul>
      {edges.map(({ node: { title } }) => (
        <li key={title}>{title}</li>
      ))}
    </ul>
  </div>
)

export const query = graphql'
  query SportsArticles {
    allArticlesJson(filter: { topic: { eq: "sports" } }) {
      edges {
        node {
          topic
          title
        }
      }
    }
  }
'
```

You might have noticed that these three components look very similar. This is because they're all working with the same data. The only unique thing about them is their title. To reduce some of this redundancy, you could create a higher-order component that takes a `name` argument and returns the same underlying component used on each page:

```
import React from 'react'
import Link from 'gatsby-link'
```

```
export default title => ({ data: { allArticlesJson: { edges } } }) => (
  <div>
    <h1>{title}</h1>
    <Link to="/">Home</Link>
    <ul>
      {edges.map(({ node: { title } }) => (
        <li key={title}>{title}</li>
      ))}
    </ul>
  </div>
)
```

Then, you could use it like this:

```
import React from 'react'
Import ArticleList from '../components/ArticleList'

export default ArticleList('Global Articles')

export const query = graphql'
  query GlobalArticles {
    allArticlesJson(filter: { topic: { eq: "global" } }) {
      edges {
        node {
          topic
          title
        }
      }
    }
  }
'
```

In order to view all of these pages, you need an index page that links to each of them:

```
import React from 'react'
import Link from 'gatsby-link'

const IndexPage = () => (
  <div>
    <h1>Home</h1>
    <p>Choose an article category</p>
    <ul>
      <li>
        <Link to="/global/">Global</Link>
      </li>
      <li>
        <Link to="/local/">Local</Link>
      </li>
```

```
      <li>
        <Link to="/sports/">Sports</Link>
      </li>
    </ul>
  </div>
)

export default IndexPage
```

Here's what the home page looks like:

If you were to click on one of the topic links, like **Global** for example, you're taken to an article list page:

Fetching remote data

Gatsby has a rich ecosystem of data source plugins—we don't have time go through all of them. It's common for a Gatsby source plugin to reach out to another system and fetch data over the network at build time. The `gatsby-source-hacker-news` plugin is a great plugin to start with, so that you can see how this fetching process works with Gatsby.

Instead of building your own Hacker News website using Gatsby, we'll use the demo created by `https://github.com/ajayns`. To get started, you can clone into his repo as follows:

```
git clone https://github.com/ajayns/gatsby-hacker-news.git
cd gatsby-hacker-news
```

Then you can install dependencies, including the `gatsby-source-hacker-news` plugin:

```
npm install
```

You don't need to edit the project configuration to enable anything, because this is already a Gatsby project. Simply start the development server as you've done throughout this chapter:

```
gatsby develop
```

Compared to other websites you've worked on this chapter, this time around the build takes longer to complete. This is due to the fact that that Gatsby has to fetch data over the network. There are also more resources to fetch. If you look at the console output from the development server, you should see the following:

```
success onPreBootstrap - 0.011 s
● starting to fetch data from the Hacker News GraphQL API. Warning, this
can take a long time e.g. 10-20 seconds
● source and transform nodesfetch HN data: 10138.119ms
```

This indicates that the build will take longer due to the work that needs to happen in order to load the Hacker News data. Once this process completes, you can load the site in your browser. You should see something similar to the following:

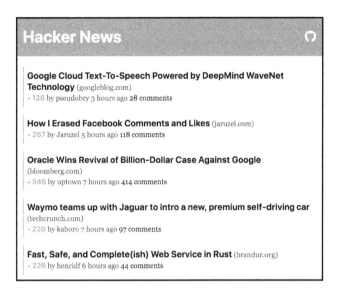

Let's take a look at the GraphQL query that loaded the data used to render this content. In the `index.js` page, you'll find the following query:

```
query PageQuery {
  allHnStory(sort: { fields: [order] }, limit: 10) {
    edges {
      node {
        ...Story
      }
    }
  }
}
```

Instead of individual node fields being specified, there's `...Story`. This is called a **fragment** and it's defined in the `StoryItem` component:

```
fragment Story on HNStory {
  id
  title
  score
  order
  domain
  url
  by
  descendants
  timeISO(fromNow: true)
}
```

The `StoryItem` component defines this GraphQL fragment because it uses this data. Now, let's shift over to GraphiQL and put this query together and execute it:

```
GraphiQL    ▶    Prettify    History                                                          < Docs

1 ▾ fragment Story on HNStory {                      ▾ {
2      id                                                "data": {
3      title                                               "allHnStory": {
4      score                                                 "edges": [
5      order                                                   {
6      domain                                                    "node": {
7      url                                                         "id": "16691203",
8      by                                                          "title": "Google Cloud Text-To-Speech Powered by
9      descendants                                       DeepMind WaveNet Technology",
10     timeISO(fromNow: true)                                      "score": 126,
11  }                                                             "order": 1,
12                                                                "domain": "googleblog.com",
13 ▾ query PageQuery {                                             "url":
14 ▾   allHnStory(sort: {fields: [order]}, limit: 10) {   "https://cloudplatform.googleblog.com/2018/03/introducing-Cloud-
15 ▾     edges {                                           Text-to-Speech-powered-by-Deepmind-WaveNet-technology.html",
16         node {                                                  "by": "pseudobry",
17           ...Story                                              "descendants": 28,
18         }                                                       "timeISO": "3 hours ago"
19       }                                                      }
20     }                                                      },
21  }                                                         {
22                                                              "node": {
                                                                 "id": "16689699",
                                                                 "title": "How I Erased Facebook Comments and Likes",
                                                                 "score": 267,
                                                                 "order": 2,
                                                                 "domain": "jaruzel.com",
                                                                 "url": "http://www.jaruzel.com/blog/How-I-Erased-
                                                       5000-Facebook-Comments-and-Likes",
                                                                 "by": "Jaruzel",
                                                                 "descendants": 118,
                                                                 "timeISO": "5 hours ago"
                                                               }
                                                             },
```

This is how the home page of the site loads data fetched from the Hack News API. Here's what the home page component looks like:

```
import React from 'react'

import StoryItem from '../components/story-item'

const IndexPage = ({ data, active }) => (
  <div>
    <div>
      {data.allHnStory.edges.map(({ node }) => (
        <StoryItem key={node.id} story={node} active={false} />
      ))}
    </div>
  </div>
)

export default IndexPage
```

The edges of the returned data are mapped to `StoryItem` components, passing in the data node. Here's what the `StoryItem` component looks like:

```
import React, { Component } from 'react';
import Link from 'gatsby-link';

import './story-item.css';

const StoryItem = ({ story, active }) => (
  <div
    className="story"
    style={active ? { borderLeft: '6px solid #ff6600' } : {}}
  >
    <div className="header">
      <a href={story.url}>
        <h4>{story.title}</h4>
      </a>
      <span className="story-domain">
        {' '}({story.domain})
      </span>
    </div>
    <div className="info">
      <h4 className="score">▲ {story.score}</h4>
      {' '}
      by <span className="author">{story.by}</span>
      {' '}
      <span className="time">{story.timeISO}</span>
      {' '}
      {active ? (
        ''
      ) : (
        <Link to={`/item/${story.id}`} className="comments">
          {story.descendants} comments
        </Link>
      )}
    </div>
  </div>
);

export default StoryItem;
```

Here you can see how this component uses the data defined by the GraphQL fragment that was passed to the larger query.

Now let's click on the comments link of a story, which will take you to the details page of a story. The new URL should look something like `http://localhost:8000/item/16691203` and the page should look something like this:

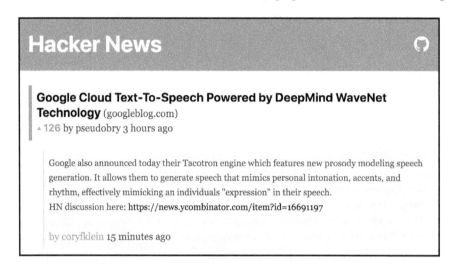

You're probably wondering where this page comes from, given that it has a URL parameter (the ID of the story). When using Gatsby to build static pages that have a dynamic URL component to them, you have to write some code whose job is to tell Gatsby how to create pages based on GraphQL query results. This code goes into the `gatsby-node.js` module. Here's how the pages in this Hacker News website are created:

```
const path = require('path')

exports.createPages = ({ graphql, boundActionCreators }) => {
  const { createPage } = boundActionCreators
  return new Promise((resolve, reject) => {
    graphql('
      {
        allHnStory(sort: { fields: [order] }, limit: 10) {
          edges {
            node {
              id
            }
          }
        }
      }
    ').then(result => {
      if (result.errors) {
```

```
      reject(result.errors)
    }

    const template = path.resolve('./src/templates/story.js')

    result.data.allHnStory.edges.forEach(({ node }) => {
      createPage({
        path: '/item/${node.id}',
        component: template,
        context: {
          id: node.id,
        },
      })
    })

    resolve()
  })
})
}
```

This module exports a `createPages()` function that Gatsby will use to create the static Hacker News article pages at build time. It starts by using the `grapghql()` function to execute a query to find all of the article nodes that you need to create pages for:

```
graphql('
  {
    allHnStory(sort: { fields: [order] }, limit: 10) {
      edges {
        node {
          id
        }
      }
    }
  }
')
```

Next, the `createPage()` function is called for each node:

```
const template = path.resolve('./src/templates/story.js')

result.data.allHnStory.edges.forEach(({ node }) => {
  createPage({
    path: '/item/${node.id}',
    component: template,
    context: {
      id: node.id,
    },
```

```
  })
})
```

The properties that are passed to `createPage()` are:

- `path`: This is the URL that when accessed, will render the page.
- `component`: This is the filesystem path to the React component that renders the page content.
- `context`: This is data that's passed to the React component. In this case, it's important that the component knows the article ID.

This is the general approach that you would take with Gatsby any time you have lots of pages to generate based on dynamic data, but the same React component can be used to render the content. In other words, you would probably rather write this code and a React component rather than separate components for every article.

Let's take a look at the component that's used to render the article details page:

```
import React from 'react'

import StoryItem from '../components/story-item'
import Comment from '../components/comment'

const Story = ({ data }) => (
  <div>
    <StoryItem story={data.hnStory} active={true} />
    <ul>
      {data.hnStory.children.map(comment => (
        <Comment key={comment.id} data={comment} />
      ))}
    </ul>
  </div>
)

export default Story

export const pageQuery = graphql'
  query StoryQuery($id: String!) {
    hnStory(id: { eq: $id }) {
      ...Story
      children {
        ...Comment
      }
    }
  }
'
```

Once again, the component relies on Gatsby executing the GraphQL query found in the `pageQuery` constant. The context is passed to `createPage()` in `gatsby-node.js`. This is how you're able to feed the `$id` argument into the query so that you can query for the specific story data.

Summary

In this chapter, you learned about Gatsby, a tool for generating static websites based on React components. We started the chapter off with a discussion on why you might want to consider building static sites, and why React is a good fit for this job. Static sites lead to an overall better user experience because they don't utilize the same types of resources as regular React apps would.

Next, you built your first Gatsby website. You learned the basic layout of files that are created by Gatsby starter templates and how to link pages together. Then, you learned that Gatsby data is driven by a plugin architecture. Gatsby is able to support various data sources via plugins. You got started with local filesystem data. Next, you learned about transformer plugins. These types of Gatsby plugins enable specific types of data sources to be queried via GraphQL.

Lastly, you looked at a Hacker News example built using Gatsby. This exposed you to fetching remote API data as the data source and generating pages dynamically based on GraphQL query results.

In the next and final chapter, you'll learn about tooling to containerize and deploy your React applications alongside the services that they consume.

11
Building and Deploying React Applications with Docker Containers

Up until this point in the book, you've been running your React applications in development mode, using the various tools that you've been learning. In this chapter, we'll switch our focus to production environment tooling. The overall aim is to be able to deploy your React application to a production environment. Thankfully, there's much tooling to help with this work, which you'll familiarize yourself with in this chapter. Your goals in this chapter are:

- Building a basic messaging React app that utilizes an API
- Using a Node container to run your React application
- Splitting your app into deployable services that run in containers
- Using static React builds for production environments

Building a messaging app

It's difficult to talk about tooling used to deploy React applications without any context. For this, you'll throw together a basic messaging app. In this section, you'll see how the app works and how it is built. Then, you'll be ready for the remaining chapter sections where you'll learn how to deploy your application as a set of containers.

The basic idea of this app is to be able to login and send messages to your contacts, as well as receiving messages. We'll keep it super simple. In terms of functionality, it'll barely match SMS capabilities. In fact, that can be the app title—*Barely SMS*. The idea is to have a React application with enough moving parts to test out in a production setting, as well as a server that you'll be able to deploy in a container later on.

For visual appearance, we'll use the Material-UI (`https://material-ui-next.com/`) component library. However, the choice of UI components should not affect the lessons of this chapter.

Starting Barely SMS

To get familiar with *Barely SMS*, let's start it up in your terminal the same way you've been doing all along in this book so far. Once you change into the `building-a-messaging-app` directory in the source code bundle that comes with this book, you can start the development server just like any other `create-react-app` project:

```
npm start
```

In another Terminal window or tab, you can start the API server for *Barely SMS* by running the following command from within the same directory:

```
npm run api
```

This will start a basic Express (`http://expressjs.com/`) app. Once the server is up and listening for requests, you should see the following output:

```
API server listening on port 3001!
```

Now you're ready to login.

Logging in

When you first load the UI, you should see the login screen that looks like this:

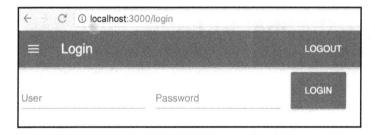

The following mock users exist as part of the API:

- user1
- user2
- user3
- user4
- user5

The password isn't actually validated against anything, so leaving it blank or entering gibberish should authenticate any of the preceding users. Let's take a look at the Login component that renders this page:

```
import React, { Component } from 'react';

import { withStyles } from 'material-ui/styles';
import TextField from 'material-ui/TextField';
import Button from 'material-ui/Button';

import { login } from './api';

const styles = theme => ({
  container: {
    display: 'flex',
    flexWrap: 'wrap'
  },
  textField: {
    marginLeft: theme.spacing.unit,
    marginRight: theme.spacing.unit,
    width: 200
  },
  button: {
    margin: theme.spacing.unit
  }
});

class Login extends Component {
  state = {
    user: '',
    password: ''
  };

  onInputChange = name => event => {
    this.setState({
      [name]: event.target.value
    });
```

```
  };

  onLoginClick = () => {
    login(this.state).then(resp => {
      if (resp.status === 200) {
        this.props.history.push('/');
      }
    });
  };

  componentWillMount() {
    this.props.setTitle('Login');
  }

  render() {
    const { classes } = this.props;
    return (
      <div className={classes.container}>
        <TextField
          id="user"
          label="User"
          className={classes.textField}
          value={this.state.user}
          onChange={this.onInputChange('user')}
          margin="normal"
        />
        <TextField
          id="password"
          label="Password"
          className={classes.textField}
          value={this.state.password}
          onChange={this.onInputChange('password')}
          type="password"
          autoComplete="current-password"
          margin="normal"
        />
        <Button
          variant="raised"
          color="primary"
          className={classes.button}
          onClick={this.onLoginClick}
        >
          Login
        </Button>
      </div>
    );
  }
}
```

```
export default withStyles(styles)(Login);
```

There's a lot of Material-UI going on here, but feel free to ignore the majority of it. The important bit is the `login()` function that's imported from the `api` module. This is used to make a call to the `/api/login` endpoint. The reason this is relevant from the perspective of production React deployment is because this is an interaction with a service that might be deployed as its own container.

The home page

If you were able to login successfully, you'll be taken to the home page of the app. You should see a page that looks like this:

The home page of *Barely SMS* shows the user's contacts who are currently online. In this case, there are clearly no other users online yet. Let's take a look at the `Home` component source now:

```
import React, { Component } from 'react';

import { withStyles } from 'material-ui/styles';
import Paper from 'material-ui/Paper';
import Avatar from 'material-ui/Avatar';
import IconButton from 'material-ui/IconButton';

import ContactMail from 'material-ui-icons/ContactMail';
import Message from 'material-ui-icons/Message';

import List, {
  ListItem,
  ListItemAvatar,
  ListItemText,
  ListItemSecondaryAction
} from 'material-ui/List';

import EmptyMessage from './EmptyMessage';
```

```
import { getContacts } from './api';

const styles = theme => ({
  root: {
    margin: '10px',
    width: '100%',
    maxWidth: 500,
    backgroundColor: theme.palette.background.paper
  }
});

class Home extends Component {
  state = {
    contacts: []
  };

  onMessageClick = id => () => {
    this.props.history.push(`/newmessage/${id}`);
  };

  componentWillMount() {
    const { setTitle, history } = this.props;

    setTitle('Barely SMS');

    const refresh = () =>
      getContacts().then(resp => {
        if (resp.status === 403) {
          history.push('/login');
        } else {
          resp.json().then(contacts => {
            this.setState({
              contacts: contacts.filter(contact => contact.online)
            });
          });
        }
      });

    this.refreshInterval = setInterval(refresh, 5000);
    refresh();
  }

  componentWillUnmount() {
    clearInterval(this.refreshInterval);
  }

  render() {
    const { classes } = this.props;
```

```
      const { contacts } = this.state;
      const { onMessageClick } = this;

      return (
        <Paper className={classes.root}>
          <EmptyMessage coll={contacts}>
            No contacts online
          </EmptyMessage>
          <List component="nav">
            {contacts.map(contact => (
              <ListItem key={contact.id}>
                <ListItemAvatar>
                  <Avatar>
                    <ContactMail />
                  </Avatar>
                </ListItemAvatar>
                <ListItemText primary={contact.name} />
                <ListItemSecondaryAction>
                  <IconButton onClick={onMessageClick(contact.id)}>
                    <Message />
                  </IconButton>
                </ListItemSecondaryAction>
              </ListItem>
            ))}
          </List>
        </Paper>
      );
    }
  }

  export default withStyles(styles)(Home);
```

In the `componentWillMount()` life cycle method, the contacts API endpoint is fetched using the `getContacts()` function. This is then repeated using an interval so that as your contacts login, they'll show up here. When the component is unmounted, the interval is cleared.

To test this, I'm going to open up Firefox (it doesn't actually matter which browser you use, as long as it's something different from where you're signed in as `user1`). From here, I can sign in as `user2`, which is a contact of `user1` and vice versa:

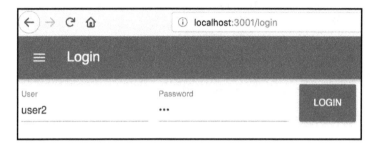

As soon as I login here, I see that **User 1** is online in another browser:

Now if I return to Chrome where I logged in as **User 1**, I should see that my **User 2** contact has signed in:

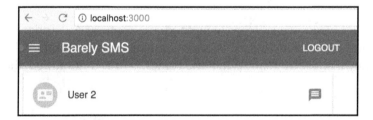

This app will follow a similar refresh pattern on other pages—an interval is used to fetch data from the API service endpoint.

The contacts page

If you want to view all of your contacts and not just those which are currently online, you have to go to the contacts page. To get there, you have to expand the navigation menu by clicking on the hamburger button to the left of the title:

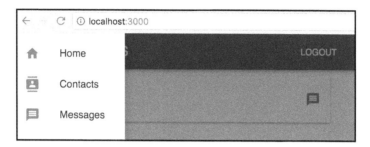

When you click on the **Contacts** link, you're taken to the contacts page which looks like this:

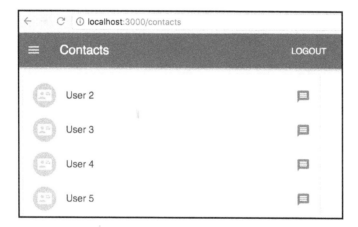

This page is very similar to the home page except that it shows all contacts. You can send a message to any user, not just those that are currently online. Let's take a look at the `Contacts` component:

```
import React, { Component } from 'react';

import { withStyles } from 'material-ui/styles';
import Paper from 'material-ui/Paper';
import Avatar from 'material-ui/Avatar';
import IconButton from 'material-ui/IconButton';

import ContactMail from 'material-ui-icons/ContactMail';
```

```
import Message from 'material-ui-icons/Message';

import List, {
  ListItem,
  ListItemAvatar,
  ListItemText,
  ListItemSecondaryAction
} from 'material-ui/List';

import EmptyMessage from './EmptyMessage';
import { getContacts } from './api';

const styles = theme => ({
  root: {
    margin: '10px',
    width: '100%',
    maxWidth: 500,
    backgroundColor: theme.palette.background.paper
  }
});

class Contacts extends Component {
  state = {
    contacts: []
  };

  onMessageClick = id => () => {
    this.props.history.push(`/newmessage/${id}`);
  };

  componentWillMount() {
    const { setTitle, history } = this.props;

    setTitle('Contacts');

    const refresh = () =>
      getContacts().then(resp => {
        if (resp.status === 403) {
          history.push('/login');
        } else {
          resp.json().then(contacts => {
            this.setState({ contacts });
          });
        }
      });

    this.refreshInterval = setInterval(refresh, 5000);
    refresh();
```

```
  }

  componentWillUnmount() {
    clearInterval(this.refreshInterval);
  }

  render() {
    const { classes } = this.props;
    const { contacts } = this.state;
    const { onMessageClick } = this;

    return (
      <Paper className={classes.root}>
        <EmptyMessage coll={contacts}>No contacts</EmptyMessage>
        <List component="nav">
          {contacts.map(contact => (
            <ListItem key={contact.id}>
              <ListItemAvatar>
                <Avatar>
                  <ContactMail />
                </Avatar>
              </ListItemAvatar>
              <ListItemText primary={contact.name} />
              <ListItemSecondaryAction>
                <IconButton onClick={onMessageClick(contact.id)}>
                  <Message />
                </IconButton>
              </ListItemSecondaryAction>
            </ListItem>
          ))}
        </List>
      </Paper>
    );
  }
}

export default withStyles(styles)(Contacts);
```

Like the `Home` component, `Contacts` uses the interval pattern to refresh contacts. For example, in the future if you wanted to add an enhancement to this page that visually indicated which users were online, you would need to have fresh data from your services.

The messages page

If you expand the navigation menu and visit the messages page, you'll see something like this:

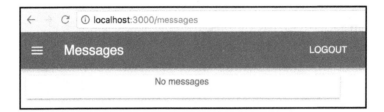

There are no messages yet. Let's take a look at the `Messages` component before sending a message:

```
import React, { Component } from 'react';
import moment from 'moment';
import { Link } from 'react-router-dom';

import { withStyles } from 'material-ui/styles';
import Paper from 'material-ui/Paper';
import Avatar from 'material-ui/Avatar';
import List, {
  ListItem,
  ListItemAvatar,
  ListItemText
} from 'material-ui/List';

import Message from 'material-ui-icons/Message';

import EmptyMessage from './EmptyMessage';
import { getMessages } from './api';

const styles = theme => ({
  root: {
    margin: '10px',
    width: '100%',
    maxWidth: 500,
    backgroundColor: theme.palette.background.paper
  }
});

class Messages extends Component {
  state = {
    messages: []
```

```
};

componentWillMount() {
  const { setTitle, history } = this.props;

  setTitle('Messages');

  const refresh = () =>
    getMessages().then(resp => {
      if (resp.status === 403) {
        history.push('/login');
      } else {
        resp.json().then(messages => {
          this.setState({
            messages: messages.map(message => ({
              ...message,
              duration: moment
                .duration(new Date() - new Date(message.timestamp))
                .humanize()
            }))
          });
        });
      }
    });

  this.refreshInterval = setInterval(refresh, 5000);
  refresh();
}

componentWillUnmount() {
  clearInterval(this.refreshInterval);
}

render() {
  const { classes } = this.props;
  const { messages } = this.state;

  return (
    <Paper className={classes.root}>
      <EmptyMessage coll={messages}>No messages</EmptyMessage>
      <List component="nav">
        {messages.map(message => (
          <ListItem
            key={message.id}
            component={Link}
            to={`/messages/${message.id}`}
          >
            <ListItemAvatar>
```

```
                <Avatar>
                  <Message />
                </Avatar>
              </ListItemAvatar>
              <ListItemText
                primary={message.fromName}
                secondary={`${message.duration} ago`}
              />
            </ListItem>
          ))}
        </List>
      </Paper>
    );
  }
}

export default withStyles(styles)(Messages);
```

Once again, the same pattern of refreshing data using an interval is in place here. When the user clicks on one of the messages, they're taken to the message details page where they can read the message content.

Sending a message

Let's go back to the other browser (Firefox in my case) where you logged in as **User 2**. Click on the little message icon beside **User 1**:

This will bring you to the new message page:

Go ahead and type a message, and hit **SEND**. Then, go back to Chrome where you're logged in as **User 1**. You should see a new message appear on the messages page from **User 2**:

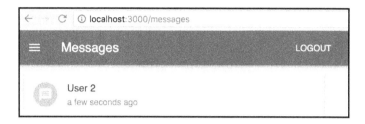

And if you click on the message, you should be able to read the message content:

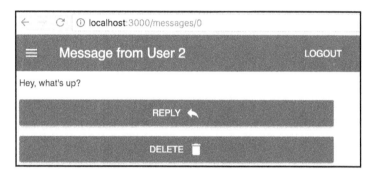

From here, you can click on the **REPLY** button to take you to the new message page, which will be addressed to **User 2** or you can delete the message. Before we look at the API code, let's take a look at the `NewMessage` component:

```
import React, { Component } from 'react';

import { withStyles } from 'material-ui/styles';
import Paper from 'material-ui/Paper';
import TextField from 'material-ui/TextField';
import Button from 'material-ui/Button';

import Send from 'material-ui-icons/Send';

import { getUser, postMessage } from './api';

const styles = theme => ({
  root: {
    display: 'flex',
    flexWrap: 'wrap',
```

```
      flexDirection: 'column'
    },
    textField: {
      marginLeft: theme.spacing.unit,
      marginRight: theme.spacing.unit,
      width: 500
    },
    button: {
      width: 500,
      margin: theme.spacing.unit
    },
    rightIcon: {
      marginLeft: theme.spacing.unit
    }
});

class NewMessage extends Component {
  state = {
    message: ''
  };

  onMessageChange = event => {
    this.setState({
      message: event.target.value
    });
  };

  onSendClick = () => {
    const { match: { params: { id } }, history } = this.props;
    const { message } = this.state;

    postMessage({ to: id, message }).then(() => {
      this.setState({ message: '' });
      history.push('/');
    });
  };

  componentWillMount() {
    const {
      match: { params: { id } },
      setTitle,
      history
    } = this.props;

    getUser(id).then(resp => {
      if (resp.status === 403) {
        history.push('/login');
      } else {
```

```
      resp.json().then(user => {
        setTitle(`New message for ${user.name}`);
      });
    }
  });
}

render() {
  const { classes } = this.props;
  const { message } = this.state;
  const { onMessageChange, onSendClick } = this;

  return (
    <Paper className={classes.root}>
      <TextField
        id="multiline-static"
        label="Message"
        multiline
        rows="4"
        className={classes.textField}
        margin="normal"
        value={message}
        onChange={onMessageChange}
      />
      <Button
        variant="raised"
        color="primary"
        className={classes.button}
        onClick={onSendClick}
      >
        Send
        <Send className={classes.rightIcon} />
      </Button>
    </Paper>
  );
}
}

export default withStyles(styles)(NewMessage);
```

Here, the `postMessage()` API function is used to send the message using the API service. Now let's look at the `MessageDetails` component:

```
import React, { Component } from 'react';
import { Link } from 'react-router-dom';

import { withStyles } from 'material-ui/styles';
```

```
import Paper from 'material-ui/Paper';
import Button from 'material-ui/Button';
import Typography from 'material-ui/Typography';

import Delete from 'material-ui-icons/Delete';
import Reply from 'material-ui-icons/Reply';

import { getMessage, deleteMessage } from './api';

const styles = theme => ({
  root: {
    display: 'flex',
    flexWrap: 'wrap',
    flexDirection: 'column'
  },
  message: {
    width: 500,
    margin: theme.spacing.unit
  },
  button: {
    width: 500,
    margin: theme.spacing.unit
  },
  rightIcon: {
    marginLeft: theme.spacing.unit
  }
});

class NewMessage extends Component {
  state = {
    message: {}
  };

  onDeleteClick = () => {
    const { history, match: { params: { id } } } = this.props;

    deleteMessage(id).then(() => {
      history.push('/messages');
    });
  };

  componentWillMount() {
    const {
      match: { params: { id } },
      setTitle,
      history
    } = this.props;
```

```
    getMessage(id).then(resp => {
      if (resp.status === 403) {
        history.push('/login');
      } else {
        resp.json().then(message => {
          setTitle(`Message from ${message.fromName}`);
          this.setState({ message });
        });
      }
    });
  }

  render() {
    const { classes } = this.props;
    const { message } = this.state;
    const { onDeleteClick } = this;

    return (
      <Paper className={classes.root}>
        <Typography className={classes.message}>
          {message.message}
        </Typography>
        <Button
          variant="raised"
          color="primary"
          className={classes.button}
          component={Link}
          to={`/newmessage/${message.from}`}
        >
          Reply
          <Reply className={classes.rightIcon} />
        </Button>
        <Button
          variant="raised"
          color="primary"
          className={classes.button}
          onClick={onDeleteClick}
        >
          Delete
          <Delete className={classes.rightIcon} />
        </Button>
      </Paper>
    );
  }
}

export default withStyles(styles)(NewMessage);
```

Here, the `getMessage()` API function is used to load the message content. Note that neither of these components use the same refresh pattern that other components have been using because the information never changes.

The API

The API is the service that your React app interacts with in order to retrieve and manipulate data. When thinking about deploying production React applications, it's important to use the API as abstraction that not only represents one service, but potentially several microservices that your application interacts with.

With that said, let's look at the API functions that are used by your React components that make up *Barely SMS*:

```
export const login = body =>
  fetch('/api/login', {
    method: 'post',
    headers: { 'Content-Type': 'application/json' },
    body: JSON.stringify(body),
    credentials: 'same-origin'
  });

export const logout = user =>
  fetch('/api/logout', {
    method: 'post',
    credentials: 'same-origin'
  });

export const getUser = id =>
  fetch(`/api/user/${id}`, { credentials: 'same-origin' });

export const getContacts = () =>
  fetch('/api/contacts', { credentials: 'same-origin' });

export const getMessages = () =>
  fetch('/api/messages', { credentials: 'same-origin' });

export const getMessage = id =>
  fetch(`/api/message/${id}`, { credentials: 'same-origin' });

export const postMessage = body =>
  fetch('/api/messages', {
    method: 'post',
    headers: { 'Content-Type': 'application/json' },
    body: JSON.stringify(body),
```

```
    credentials: 'same-origin'
  });

export const deleteMessage = id =>
  fetch(`/api/message/${id}`, {
    method: 'delete',
    credentials: 'same-origin'
  });
```

These simple abstractions use `fetch()` to make HTTP requests to the API services. Right now, there's only one API service running as a single process that has mock user data and all changes happen in memory only—nothing is persisted:

```
const express = require('express');
const bodyParser = require('body-parser');
const cookieParser = require('cookie-parser');

const sessions = [];
const messages = [];
const users = {
  user1: {
    name: 'User 1',
    contacts: ['user2', 'user3', 'user4', 'user5'],
    online: false
  },
  user2: {
    name: 'User 2',
    contacts: ['user1', 'user3', 'user4', 'user5'],
    online: false
  },
  user3: {
    name: 'User 3',
    contacts: ['user1', 'user2', 'user4', 'user5'],
    online: false
  },
  user4: {
    name: 'User 4',
    contacts: ['user1', 'user2', 'user3', 'user5'],
    online: false
  },
  user5: {
    name: 'User 5',
    contacts: ['user1', 'user2', 'user3', 'user4']
  }
};

const authenticate = (req, res, next) => {
```

```
    if (!sessions.includes(req.cookies.session)) {
      res.status(403).end();
    } else {
      next();
    }
};

const app = express();
app.use(cookieParser());
app.use(bodyParser.json());
app.use(bodyParser.urlencoded({ extended: true }));

app.post('/api/login', (req, res) => {
  const { user } = req.body;

  if (users.hasOwnProperty(user)) {
    sessions.push(user);
    users[user].online = true;
    res.cookie('session', user);
    res.end();
  } else {
    res.status(403).end();
  }
});

app.post('/api/logout', (req, res) => {
  const { session } = req.cookies;
  const index = sessions.indexOf(session);

  sessions.splice(index, 1);
  users[session].online = false;

  res.clearCookie('session');
  res.status(200).end();
});

app.get('/api/user/:id', authenticate, (req, res) => {
  res.json(users[req.params.id]);
});

app.get('/api/contacts', authenticate, (req, res) => {
  res.json(
    users[req.cookies.session].contacts.map(id => ({
      id,
      name: users[id].name,
      online: users[id].online
    }))
  );
```

```
  });

  app.post('/api/messages', authenticate, (req, res) => {
    messages.push({
      from: req.cookies.session,
      fromName: users[req.cookies.session].name,
      to: req.body.to,
      message: req.body.message,
      timestamp: new Date()
    });

    res.status(201).end();
  });

  app.get('/api/messages', authenticate, (req, res) => {
    res.json(
      messages
        .map((message, id) => ({ ...message, id }))
        .filter(message => message.to === req.cookies.session)
    );
  });

  app.get('/api/message/:id', authenticate, (req, res) => {
    const { params: { id } } = req;
    res.json({ ...messages[id], id });
  });

  app.delete('/api/message/:id', authenticate, (req, res) => {
    messages.splice(req.params.id, 1);
    res.status(200).end();
  });

  app.listen(3001, () =>
    console.log('API server listening on port 3001!')
  );
```

This is an Express app that keeps app data in simple JavaScript objects and arrays. While everything happens within this one service now, that might not always be the case. Some of these API calls might live in different services. This is what makes deploying to containers so powerful—you can abstract complex deployments at a high level.

Getting started with Node containers

Let's start things off by running the *Barely SMS* React dev server within a Node.js Docker image. Note that this is not part of the production deployment. This is just a starting point for you to get familiar with deploying Docker containers. As we progress through the remaining sections in this chapter, you'll move steadily toward a production-level deployment.

The first step to getting your React application into a container is creating a `Dockerfile`. If you don't have Docker installed on your system already, find it here along with installation instructions: `https://www.docker.com/community-edition`. If you open up a terminal and change into the `getting-started-with-containers` directory, you'll see a file called `Dockerfile`. Here's what it looks like:

```
FROM node:alpine
WORKDIR /usr/src/app
COPY package*.json ./
RUN npm install
COPY . .
EXPOSE 3000
CMD [ "npm", "start" ]
```

This is the file that's used to build an image. An image is like a template for the container process that runs your React application. Essentially, these lines do the following:

- `FROM node:alpine`: What's the base image that this image uses. This is a small version of Linux with Node.js on it.
- `WORKDIR /usr/src/app`: Changes the working directory on the container.
- `COPY package*.json ./`: Copies `package.json` and `package-lock.json` to the container.
- `RUN npm install`: Installs npm package dependencies on the container.
- `COPY . .`: Copies the source code of your app to the container.
- `EXPOSE 3000`: Exposes port 3000 when the container is running.
- `CMD [ "npm", "start" ]`: Runs `npm start` when the container starts.

The next file that you'll want to add is a `.dockerignore` file. This file lists everything that you don't want included on the image by the `COPY` command. Here's what it looks like:

```
node_modules
npm-debug.log
```

It's important that you don't copy over npm_modules that you might have installed on your system because the npm install command will install them again and you'll have two copies of your libs.

Before you build the Docker image that you can deploy, there are a couple of minor changes to make. First, you need to figure out what your IP address is so that you can use it to communicate with the API server. You can find it by running ifconfig in your terminal. Once you have it, you can update the proxy value in package.json. It used to be:

```
http://localhost:3001
```

Now it should have an IP address so that your Docker container can reach it once it's running. Here's what mine looks like:

```
http://192.168.86.237:3001
```

Next, you'll want to pass your IP as an argument to the listen() method in server.js. It used to be:

```
app.listen(3001, () =>
  console.log('API server listening on port 3001!')
);
```

Here's what mine looks like now:

```
app.listen(3001, '192.168.86.237', () =>
  console.log('API server listening on port 3001!')
);
```

Now you're ready to build the Docker image by running the following command:

```
docker build -t barely-sms-ui .
```

This will build an image with the ID barely-sms-ui using the Dockerfile found in the current directory. Once built, you can see the image by running docker images. The output should look something like this:

```
REPOSITORY      TAG      IMAGE ID       CREATED       SIZE
barely-sms-ui   latest   b1526915598d   7 hours ago   267MB
```

Now you're ready to deploy the container with the following command:

```
docker run -p 3000:3000 barely-sms-ui
```

To cleanup old unused containers, you can run the following command:

```
docker system prune
```

The `-p 3000:3000` argument ensures that the exposed port, `3000`, on the container is mapped to port `3000` on your system. You can test this by opening `http://localhost:3000/`. However, you might see an error that looks like this:

```
←  →   1 of 2 errors on the page                                                              ×

Unhandled Rejection (SyntaxError): Unexpected token P in JSON at position 0

(anonymous function)
src/app/src/Home.js:49

  46 |  if (resp.status === 403) {
  47 |    history.push('/login');
  48 |  } else {
> 49 |    resp.json().then(contacts => {
  50 |      this.setState({
  51 |        contacts: contacts.filter(contact => contact.online)
  52 |      });
```

And if you look at the container console output, you'll see something that looks like the following:

```
    Proxy error: Could not proxy request /api/contacts from localhost:3000
to http://192.168.86.237:3001.
    See https://nodejs.org/api/errors.html#errors_common_system_errors for
more information (ECONNREFUSED).
```

This is because you haven't started the API server yet. You'll actually see a similar error if you put an invalid IP address as a proxy address. If you have or you need to change the proxy value for whatever reason, you'll have to rebuild the image and then restart the container. If you start the API by running `npm run api` in another terminal and then reload the UI, everything should work as expected.

Composing React apps with services

The main challenge with the previous section was that you had a user interface service self-contained as a running container. The API service, on the other hand, was off doing its own thing. The next tool that you'll learn how to use is `docker-compose`. As the name suggests, `docker-compose` is how you compose larger applications out of smaller services. The next natural step for *Barely SMS* is to use this Docker tool to make the API service and to control both services as one application.

This time, we'll need two `Dockerfile` files. You can reuse the `Dockerfile` from the preceding section—just rename it to `Dockerfile.ui`. Then, create another `Dockerfile` that's nearly identical—call it `Dockerfile.api` and give it the following contents:

```
FROM node:alpine
WORKDIR /usr/src/app
COPY package*.json ./
RUN npm install
COPY . .
EXPOSE 3001
CMD [ "npm", "run", "api" ]
```

The two differences are the `EXPOSE` port value and the `CMD` that is run. This command starts the API server instead of the React development server.

Before you build the images, the `server.js` and `package.js` files need minor adjustments. In `package.json`, the proxy can simply point to `http://api:3001`. In `server.js`, make sure that you're no longer passing a specific IP address to `listen()`:

```
app.listen(3001, () =>
  console.log('API server listening on port 3001!')
);
```

Building the two images requires a slight modification as well because you're no longer using the standard name for the `Dockerfile`. Here's how to build the UI image:

```
docker build -f Dockerfile.ui -t barely-sms-ui .
```

Then, build the API image:

```
docker build -f Dockerfile.api -t barely-sms-api .
```

At this point, you're ready to create a `docker-compose.yml`. This is how you declare what the `docker-compose` tool should do when invoked. Here's what it looks like:

```
api:
  image: barely-sms-api
  expose:
    - 3001
  ports:
    - "3001:3001"
ui:
  image: barely-sms-ui
  expose:
    - 3000
  links:
    - api
  ports:
    - "3000:3000"
```

As you can see, this YAML markup is clearly separated into two services. First there's the `api` service, which points to the `barely-sms-api` image and maps ports accordingly. Then, there's the `ui` service, which does the same thing except that it points to the `barely-sms-ui` image and maps to different ports. It also links to the API service because you want to make sure that the API service is available before the UI is loaded in any browser.

To bring the services up, you can run the following command:

```
docker-compose up
```

You should then see logs from bother services in your console. Then, if you visit `http://localhost:3000/`, you should be able to use *Barely SMS* as you normally would, except this time, everything is self-contained. From this point forward, you're in a better position to grow your application as the requirements evolve. As necessary, you can add new services and have your React components talk to them like they're all talking to the same application while keeping the services modular and self-contained.

Static React builds for production

The final step to making *Barely SMS* ready for production deployment is removing the React development server from the UI service. The development server was never intended for production use because it has many parts that aid developers, but ultimately slow down the overall user experience and have no place in a production environment.

Instead of using a Node.js based image, you can use a simple NGINX HTTP server that serves static content. Since this is a production environment and you don't need a development server that builds UI assets on the fly, you can just use the `create-react-app` build script to build your static artifacts for NGINX to serve:

```
npm run build
```

Then, you can change the `Dockerfile.ui` file so that it looks like this:

```
FROM nginx:alpine
EXPOSE 3000
COPY nginx.conf /etc/nginx/nginx.conf
COPY build /data/www
CMD ["nginx", "-g", "daemon off;"]
```

This time, the image is basic on an NGINX server that serves static content, and we're passing it a `nginx.conf` file. Here's what this looks like:

```
worker_processes 2;

events {
  worker_connections 2048;
}

http {
  upstream service_api {
    server api:3001;
  }

  server {
    location / {
      root /data/www;
      try_files $uri /index.html;
    }

    location /api {
      proxy_pass http://service_api;
    }
  }
}
```

Here you have a fine-grained level of control over where HTTP requests are sent. For example, if the `/api/login` and `/api/logout` endpoints were moved to their own service, you could control this change here rather than having to rebuild the UI image.

The last change that's required to be done is to `docker-compose.yml`:

```
api:
  image: barely-sms-api
  expose:
    - 3001
  ports:
    - "3001:3001"

ui:
  image: barely-sms-ui
  expose:
    - 80
  links:
    - api
  ports:
    - "3000:80"
```

Did you notice that port `3000` now maps to port `80` in the `ui` service? This is because NGINX serves on port `80`. If you run `docker-compose up`, you should be able to visit `http://localhost:3000/` and interact with your static build.

Congratulations! With no more React development server, you're just about as ready for production as you can be from a build tool perspective.

Summary

In this chapter, you built a simple messaging app called *Barely SMS*. Then, you learned how to deploy this app as a Docker container. Then, you learned how to package services together, including the UI service, so that you have a higher level of abstraction to work with when deploying applications with many moving parts. Lastly, you learned how to build production-ready static assets and serve them with an industrial strength HTTP server—NGINX.

I hope this has been an enlightening read. It was both a challenge and a joy to write. Tooling in web development shouldn't be as difficult as it has been over the past decade. Projects like React and browser vendors like Chrome are starting to change this trend. I believe that any technology is only as good as its tooling. Now that you have a firm handle on tooling available in the React ecosystem, put it to good use and let it do the hard work for you.

Another Book You May Enjoy

If you enjoyed this book, you may be interested in another book by Packt:

React 16 Essentials - Second Edition
Artemij Fedosejev, Adam Boduch

ISBN: 978-1-78712-604-6

- Learn to code React 16 with hands-on examples and clear tutorials
- Install powerful React 16 tools to make development much more efficient
- Understand the impact of React Fiber today and the future of your web development
- Utilize the Redux application architecture with your React components
- Create React 16 elements with properties and children
- Get started with stateless and stateful React components
- Use JSX to speed up your React 16 development process
- Add reactivity to your React 16 components with lifecycle methods
- Test your React 16 components with the Jest test framework

Leave a review – let other readers know what you think

Please share your thoughts on this book with others by leaving a review on the site that you bought it from. If you purchased the book from Amazon, please leave us an honest review on this book's Amazon page. This is vital so that other potential readers can see and use your unbiased opinion to make purchasing decisions, we can understand what our customers think about our products, and our authors can see your feedback on the title that they have worked with Packt to create. It will only take a few minutes of your time, but is valuable to other potential customers, our authors, and Packt. Thank you!

Index

www.ingramcontent.com/pod-product-compliance
Lightning Source LLC
Chambersburg PA
CBHW080629060326
40690CB00021B/4859